Development and Administration of Education in Uganda

J. C. Ssekamwa
S. M. E. Lugumba

Fountain Publishers

Fountain Publishers
P.O. Box 488
Kampala

© J. C. Ssekamwa 1971, 2001
First published 1971
Second edition by Fountain Publishers 2000

All rights reserved. No part of this publication may be reproduced, stored in a retrieval system or transmitted in any form or by any means electronic, mechanical, photocopying, recording or otherwise without the prior written permission of the publisher.

ISBN 9970 02 246 6

Cataloguing-in-publication data

Ssekamwa J.C. and Lugumba S.M.
Development of Education in Uganda
ISBN 9970 02 246 6
1. History – Uganda   2. Education – Uganda
I. Title
390.9676

Contents

Introduction		ii
Part One:	**Development of Education in Uganda**	1
1:	Education in Uganda 1900-1970	2
Part Two:	**The Task and Challenge of the Development of Teacher Education**	21
2:	Teacher Education to 1925 and after	
3:	Training of Teachers for Secondary Schools ups and downs, 1953-1970	31
4:	The Teacher in Uganda, Past and Present	39
Part Three:	**Educational Administration: Practices and Trends**	
5:	The Structure of the Education System	55
6:	Administration at Ministry and District levels	63
7:	Administration: School level (Secondary)	78
References		92
Appendices		
A:	*Directors of Education 1925 - 1962*	94
	Education officers 1962 - 1970	94
	Chief Inspectors of Schools 1934 - 1972	94
B:	*Secondary Schools 1972*	94
	Schools with S1 - S6 classes	94
	Schools with S1 - S4 classes	95
Index		97

Introduction

After serious research, the late Sera Erunasani Mugumba Lugumba and myself set out to write an account of the development of education in Uganda between 1900 and 1970 entitled *Educational Development and Administration in Uganda.* The book was published in 1971. We wanted to record the most salient developments in the field of education in this country during that time so that posterity might read about them, more especially because both of us had for the largest part of that period lived through them. On editing this edition of the book, it has struck me that we were very shrewd indeed to have decided to write the account which is contained in the book.

Today's structure of education in Uganda and the administrative set-up have both changed drastically - so that a person who reads this book might wonder whether he or she is not reading about a different education system altogether. Indeed this emphasises the words of one of my Professors of History, J.B. Webster. He said that "every knowledgeable old African person who gets buried is Africa's history lost." The lesson from that professor's message was that all knowledgeable people who have been blessed with longevity should try to commit to writing events which have influenced the course of the bit of history they remember; also that those historians who can, should seek out those old knowledgeable persons and record from them what is worth recording about the past before their bones are interred.

Professor Webster was quite correct. My colleague, the late Sera Lugumba, departed from this world in 1992, having participated usefully in the recording of the events that built up this coherent story of the development of the education system in Uganda between 1900 and 1970.

The late Sera Lugumba was older than me. Thus the beauty of this history is that it was recorded by people who went through that system of education and who could therefore give an eyewitness account of what happened then.

The events which are described in this book stop around the mid 1970s. The events that occurred between that time and today are recorded in a book entitled *History and Development of Education in Uganda*, written by only myself, my colleague Sera Lugumba having passed away by the time I wrote it.

I would like to end this introduction by paying tribute to the late Sera Erunasani Mugumba Lugumba. Both of us were an inspiration to each other and shared great fun while reflecting on the events described in this book because we had lived through them.

J.C. Ssekamwa
School of Education
Makerere University
2001

PART ONE

DEVELOPMENT OF EDUCATION IN UGANDA

1

Education in Uganda 1900 - 1970

The period 1900 - 1925

Until 1925, practically all education was in the hands of the Protestant and Catholic missions. With the exception of some buildings erected at Makerere by the Protectorate Government as a school to train mechanics and carpenters and a few centres where medical workers were trained, all school buildings and teachers in the country belonged to the missionary groups. Without the assistance of the government, they laid the foundations and accepted the challenge of heavy and testing commitments. What goals did the missionaries wish to achieve?

At first, the effort of the missionaries was focused on making their converts literate so that they could refresh their religious knowledge in their homes by reading books provided by the missions. However, by 1901, the missionaries had recognised the need of a form of education designed to help build the character of the pupils and to prepare them for a wider world in which they would live. It was felt that this aim could best be realised through boarding school education, using English as the medium of instruction.

The first school along such lines was started at Namilyango 12 miles away from Kampala by Mill Hill Fathers in 1902. The first batch of students were the sons of chiefs. In addition to the three R's, taught English Grammar, Geography, Maths, Music and Games. After Namilyango College, many other schools of a similar type were opened. Among these were Mengo High School 1903, Gayaza High School 1905, King's College, Budo 1906, Kamuli, Kisubi, Mbarara and Bukalasa. The majority of these schools were mainly for sons and daughters of more influential families. This was acceptable to contemporaries.

By the year 1924, when the Phelps-Stokes Commission visited Uganda, missionaries operated six types of schools:
(i) Colleges, e.g. Kisubi, Namilyango, Budo
(ii) Normal schools - for training teachers.
(iii) High schools - usually boarding with a high level of efficiency maintained and headed by a European. The standard was about that of primary seven or junior secondary.
(iv) Central schools - day schools providing rudimentary education.
(v) Subgrade - of uncertain educational value - no staff and no supervision.
(vi) Maternity schools - these trained midwives. It would be safe to say that, generally speaking, missionaries had some sort of institution in the majority of the districts comprising Uganda. However, while they did their utmost to

improve educational facilities, their overzealous approach to religion meant that their institutions produced educated Roman Catholics or Protestants rather than educated Ugandans.

The Phelps-Stokes Commission 1924, reports on education in Uganda.
In 1924, Trustees of the Phelps-Stokes Fund (USA), sent a team of ten educational experts to tour tropical Africa to find out:
(a) What and how much educational work was being done for the Africans in each of the territories visited.
(b) The educational needs of the people with reference to religious, social, hygienic and economic conditions, to ascertain the extent to which these needs were being met, and to make suggestions as to how they might best be met. The Commission was asked to publish its findings.

The Commission visited the Protectorate in 1924. It gave credit to the missionaries and staff for having made a good start in despite of very limited funds and observed that a lot remained to be done. It was felt that much of the weakness of the education system in Uganda was due to the absence of a government department of education and government inspectors of schools. Therefore, it was recommended that the Protectorate Government set up a Department of Education without further delay. Concerned that the missionaries had failed to relate their educational activities to the needs of the people, the commissioners in the recommendations stressed the needs of the pupil and the needs of the community. The Commission was very critical of the free use of high-sounding names for schools whose actual standard was far below what the name would suggest. It recommended that a new classification, with Makerere at the top, be undertaken.

Missionaries' contribution to education up to 1925
As already mentioned, the Phelps-Stokes Commission criticised the missionaries. Other people have also criticised the missionaries. Three main criticisms have been made. Firstly, that the missionaries provided education that was exclusively literary. But it seems this is an over-statement. It is not true that missionaries provided exclusively literary education. First of all, manual work was obligatory in all mission schools. Secondly, missions were the pioneers of industrial work in schools. They taught carpentry, building and printing. It is also hard to expect the missionaries, painfully short of funds, to have mounted technical training on a large scale: They just couldn't finance it.

The second criticism has been that their school system lacked supervision. This was true. They just did not have the staff to do it. Finally, the third criticism has been that their schools were detached from the common life of the people. The point made here being that, instead of making a pupil want to live in his village after he had been to school, mission schools tended to make him fit to live only as a clerk in town. This is a serious criticism but it is difficult to see how the missions could have given a technical and agricultural education to thousands of pupils in their schools without any adequate funds. As many people may know, it is often difficult to get pupils to return to the land after their schooling is finished.

Considering that missionaries were assisted only with very small annual grants from the government and, therefore, lacked adequate funds, they did a tremendous amount of work for which they deserve credit. What they achieved can be briefly summarised thus:

(i) Through their efforts, the country was covered with a network of schools. Although some of these were far from what a school should be, they at least provided a basis for future developments.
(ii) They aroused popular interest in education among boys, girls and parents.
(iii) Generally speaking, although educational advance was slow, it was broadly based.
(iv) Their school system made provision for pupils, who were able to do so, to move from the lowest to the highest rung.
(v) They established an intimate link between religion and education.
(vi) They provided the administration with trained clerical staff.

Government begins to participate in Uganda's education.
Partly as a result of the Report and recommendations of the Phelps-Stokes Commission and partly as a result of the publication of the British Government White Paper on Education in Tropical Africa of 1923, which urged close attention to education, the Protectorate Government realised that it was its duty to take a more direct part in solving the difficult problems of Uganda's education, which was by no standard adequate.

The Governor, Sir Geoffrey Archer, therefore, set up a Department of Education in 1925 with the aid of a scheme for the participation of government in education which Mr. Eric J. Hussey, Chief Inspector of Schools in Sudan, had submitted to him in August 1924 after the study he had undertaken at the Governor's request. Hussey was seconded from Sudan for service in Uganda and took up his duties as the Director of Education on 15 February 1925. Eric Hussey's arrival marked the beginning of the Ugandan Government's involvement in education. The Government's move was not welcome in some quarters. Some Europeans objected to increased expenditure on African education that would result from the Government's direct participation. Some Africans wondered what the government's motives were for interfering in a field that had been worked by missionaries alone for such a long time. The missionaries, however, warmly welcomed the move and their leaders spared no effort to impress on the doubters that Government participation would provide resources that would give education a big leap forward.

In addition to the opening of the Department of Education, what was called an Advisory Council on Native Education had been set up by March 1925. By June, this Council included all provincial commissioners and representatives of the missions as members.

Under Hussey's direction, schools throughout the country were carefully graded as follows:
(i) Subgrade schools. Schools in this category were not required to conform to a syllabus prescribed by the Government.
(ii) Elementary Vernacular schools. All schools in this group were required to use and strictly follow the syllabus as laid down by the Government. Each school of this type was required to maintain a school garden for the purpose of instructing pupils in elementary agriculture to prepare them to live in the villages.
(iii) Intermediate schools A and B. The most advanced schools of the missionaries were in the category labelled Intermediate B; they were by name, Kisubi, Budo and Namilyango. Central and High schools were labelled Intermediate A, and there were many of them.
(iv) Special grades. Technical schools and Normal schools were in this class. Normal schools trained teachers.
(v) Makerere College: the highest institution where professional courses were taken and where teachers for Intermediate schools would be trained.

Before the beginning of 1926, the majority of existing high and central schools were inspected. During the year, there was large scale adjustment and change for missions. New names had to be adopted and classes had to be adjusted to the new prescribed syllabuses. All this seems to have gone on so smoothly that the Director of Education was in a position to introduce the first Education Bill into the Legislative Council in December 1927.

The Education Ordinance 1927

By the provisions of this Ordinance, which the Director of Education described as an Ordinance to provide for development and regulation of education, the whole education system was brought under Government direction and control. However, the Government was not the owner and manager of schools. Because of the Ordinance, the government could direct and determine what the owners could do in their schools and train teachers to whom they could give employment.

The Ordinance empowered the Director of Education to register and classify all institutions at his discretion, to close schools not meeting the required standard, to impose fines on those who contravened the Ordinance, to register teachers if they passed the examinations he prescribed, and to strike any teacher off the register for repeated misconduct. He had power, according to the Ordinance, to visit any school at any time without notice and inspect it; anyone obstructing him would be liable to a fine of Shs. 1000/-. Provincial and Districts Boards, which the Ordinance set up and which were presided over by Administrative Officers, supervised schools.

While missions welcomed the Ordinance to the extent that it would give them assistance in the huge task of building, financing, staffing schools, and in training teachers and while they expressed willingness to use their influence to make it acceptable and workable, they, however, wanted its enforcement delayed, criticism encouraged, and be responded to by way of accepting amendments. They were also particularly unhappy about its penal clauses and stressed that co-operation, rather than fear of penalty, would make the law workable and respected. The Ordinance came into force on 1 September 1928. In spite of the law which gave a considerable amount of power over the school system to the Government, the ownership and management of schools remained in the hands of the mission groups. Hussey, the Director of Education, had at first hoped that mission central and high schools might be taken over by his department. He soon found out that the colonial policy did not provide for this. Indeed, until Uganda's independence in 1962, the Protectorate Government, as far as possible, confined its role in primary and secondary education by making grants to the missions, teacher-training and undertaking general overall supervision.

What type of education should schools provide? What should be the medium of instruction?

In the period 1925-1935, these two questions were important and generated a lot of discussion that gave rise to interesting experiments.

At the Legislative Council meeting of 28 May 1926, Mr H. H. Hunter a member of the Council, asked the Director of Education what steps were being taken by his department to train Ugandans in the skilled processes associated with the farming and planning industries. Hunter also wanted to know whether there was any scheme of apprenticeship for Ugandans desiring to learn skilled trades drawn up by the Education Department. These questions indicate the feeling of a small group of people, which included men like Hunter and a number of educators in the field and the Department of Education, that the education system for Ugandans should avoid too much academic training, as far as possible, but should provide vocational education and prepare the majority of the pupils to live successfully in their villages. In his reply to Mr Hunter, the Director of Education indicated that the syllabus drawn up by his department for elementary vernacular schools, for example, provided two hours of practical training in agriculture. A special agricultural course, organised by an Agricultural Officer selected by the Director of Agriculture, would be an integral part of the curriculum for the teachers' schools for training elementary school teachers. Agriculture would also figure prominently in the syllabus for higher schools. He also revealed that in the five year programme of educational development there was provision for a technical school for training apprentices in various trades. He further said that the General Manager of Kenya and Uganda Railways was willing to arrange for boys to be apprenticed to skilled workmen in his department.

Eric Hussey was a firm believer in vocational training and was openly anxious to cut down the number of mission schools which gave the usual academic training and to encourage the development of many post-primary schools into semi-vocational central schools. In the view of the Education Department under Hussey's influence, the central schools, as they were called, were the most needed post-primary institutions for Uganda which would absorb the bulk of the number of pupils leaving the elementary vernacular schools. Consequently, a number of central schools were opened and attempts made to run vocational courses. What were these central schools like?

Fully developed central schools were post-elementary semi-vocational schools offering a 3-year or 4-year course to students for whom these schools were terminal. English was taught as a subject. Otherwise, the medium of instruction was either Kiswahili or, where possible, the vernacular of the area where the school was situated. There were, on the time table, periods for agriculture, handiwork, elementary clerical and commercial studies (for example, typing). It was at one point even proposed to open and run shops at these schools to enable boys to get some practical idea of retail business. From 1935 teachers for these schools were mainly recruited from Kampala Normal School of which there is an account later in this book.

Missionaries, and articulate African opinion, while appreciative of the value of practical and manual education, considered it an inadequate preparation for leadership and the career needs of the pupils; they opposed central schools. Obviously, it is hard to believe that practical and manual education would provide inadequate preparation for leadership. The central school experiment was generally abandoned soon after 1936.

It is also hard to attach weight to the impression some people have that in the colonial period, practical education was not provided for in the school programme. Up to 1939, at least, primary schools and secondary schools had school gardens and , wherever possible, a school had a teacher who had been to a course at Bukalasa or Serere to help teach agriculture at school. Schools like King's College, Budo had what was called 'the school farm' up to the 1950s. Besides including agriculture in the curriculum for schools, there were farm schools established by the Government at Bukalasa, Serere and Masindi which ran courses that were even attended by chiefs, in the hope that they would help to spread better methods of farming in areas under their operation. No one could honestly say that work on school gardens was popular with the pupils. It was not for the simple reason that digging with a hoe is no light job and is particularly arduous for young pupils. Furthermore, often interest that might have been generated and kept running was killed when teachers punished pupils by making them dig for certain periods in the school garden. It is well to point out, further, that parents, too, did not expect their children to be cultivators like themselves. They wanted them to take up clerical work or a job less exacting than digging and one that carried prestige after they left school.

It may also be added here that when the owners of schools were encouraged by the Department of Education to experiment with giving a more practical education at the middle school level to the majority of their pupils, in order to prepare them to live in villages, some of them did so with considerable zeal. Nyakasura School, under its Headmaster, Commander E. Callwell, had perhaps the greatest success with the experiment. The school ran and maintained an electricity plant, laid on a water supply, ran courses in building and brick-making. Nor should the farm schools set up by the Protestant and Catholic missions, at Namutamba and Gulu, respectively, be forgotten.

In 1938, the schools were classified again and the system set up then has, with very little modification, existed up to now. There were to be three types of institutions after 1938.

(i) Primary School. This provided a six year course, and English was the medium of instruction from form five.
(ii) Junior Secondary School. A three year course was provided.
(iii) Senior Secondary School. This offered a three year course.

After successfully completing the Senior Secondary course and passing the entrance exams, students would proceed to Makerere College, an inter-territorial college for East Africa. Vocational education was to be provided by Technical Schools and gradually courses in commercial studies were phased out of Secondary Schools.

What should be the medium of instruction?
To some people Kiswahili seemed to be the answer to this question. In his communication to the Secretary of State for the Colonies, for example, the Governor expressed the opinion that Kiswahili be adopted for the purpose of African elementary education, for use in Normal schools in the Protectorate, and that Kiswahili be the language of instruction in the technical schools. Advocates of Kiswahili as a medium of instruction did not lack convincing arguments. They argued that there would certainly be advantages accruing from using what could easily become a lingua franca over East Africa.

The possession of a common language, they further argued, would give rise to better understanding between Ugandans and Europeans, as local dialects were too many and very few Europeans knew any reasonable number of them. Hussey, the Director of Education, who argued consistently and persuasively for the use of Kiswahili, saw in it a medium of inter-tribal and inter-territorial communication. He felt that the Kiswahili language zone would be so wide that it would give impetus to the production of reading materials.

Books in Kiswahili would be accessible to all literate East Africans whereas, if they were in English, they would be read only by those who had been to schools and learnt English. All the arguments advanced in support of the use of Kiswahili, it seems, were sound although no one, Hussey included, explained to what extent Kiswahili facilitated learning. Would pupils learn faster and more effectively when taught in Kiswahili rather than in their vernacular, for instance?

Among those who were opposed to the use of Kiswahili in schools was Mr Rowling of the CMS, Namirembe, who expressed the fear that widespread use of that language, would increase Muslim influence, and he labelled the move a political expedient. That Rowling should have taken this position is understandable: he had written quite a number of books in Luganda for which he and his supporters wrongly claimed flexibility and capability to meet the requirements of the school curriculum. Educators like H. M. Grace, headmaster of Budo, supported use of English which they naturally regarded as the gateway to knowledge and as the likely lingua franca for the educated East Africans without belittling the value of Kiswahili. But what about East Africans other than the 'elite'?

The debate went beyond the boundaries of Uganda for, in May 1931, at the meeting of the joint Parliamentary Committee on Closer Union of Kenya and Uganda, after the Ugandan witnesses had unanimously preferred English to Kiswahili as the universal language for the country, it was indicated that English would be the lingua franca in future; and so it is. However, Kiswahili was taught as a second language according to a ruling of the Department of English in Teso, Lango, Acholi, and West Nile and elsewhere as a subject, if so desired.

The period 1939 - 45 - the war time period.

As part of the British Empire, the Uganda Protectorate became involved in the Second World War as soon as it began. There was some dislocation of the education system which, fortunately, did not give rise to serious results. About nineteen European missionaries were called up and about sixty-nine missionaries and forty-nine nuns who were nationals of countries with which Britain was at war were interned. Except for the Gulu Farm School, which closed down because of the internement of the European instructor, other places did not close down as arrangements were made for them to be administered by the Educational Secretary General for Catholic mission schools. There was also loss of revenue from overseas and a reduction in the purchasing power of grants. It is, therefore, safe to say that generally the school system did not suffer undue dislocation.

The war showed how schools can be used as vehicles of information for the community and as sources for direct contributions to services required by the government.

(i) The Department of Education in conjunction with the Government Information Officer distributed news bulletins concerning the international situation to a number of schools for the eventual transmission to the homes of various communities.

(ii) Senior students of Kampala Technical School, supervised by their teachers, inspected and re-conditioned a considerable number of motor-vehicles requisitioned for war, built no less than sixty lorry-bodies, and completed and painted two hundred lorries.

(iii) Boy scouts took part in guarding Kampala, thus relieving the police.
(iv) Some schools, under the direction of the Agricultural Department, cultivated commercial crops on what were styled 'War Acres'. Revenue from the sale of the crops was paid into the Uganda War Fund. By the end of 1941, the school contribution through this means was Shs. 20,000/=.
(v) Recruiting authorities from East African army headquarters, requested and enlisted boys who had completed full primary or junior secondary courses as they were needed for semi-technical and technical sections of the army.
(vi) Some African teachers of Makerere and primary standard were recruited, particularly in the period 1940 - 41, for service with the East African Army Education Corps, to teach African languages and methods of dealing with African soldiers to European officers.
(vii) From January 1942, the mechanical section of Kampala Technical School was taken over by the army in order to turn out military artisans at the rate of 100 every three months; motor vehicle fillers, blacksmiths, tin smiths and electricians were thus produced.

During the war period, an important law concerning education was made; a brief account of which will be given here.

The 1942 Education Ordinance

In force for fifteen years, the 1927 Education Ordinance certainly needed revision; this was carried out in December 1942.

One of the more important features of the 1942 Ordinance was that section 56 in which the Governor was given the authority to prescribe the conditions governing the award of grants in-aid. By virtue of the provision, in December 1943, the self-governing schools (Grant-in-Aid) rules were made to apply to all schools receiving Grant-in-Aid from public funds. The grant-in-aid was calculated on the basis of the school's estimated revenue and budget, and it was intended to cover maintenance not covered by revenue from other sources.

The rules spelt out how such schools would be managed. There were to be Boards of Governors to control the education policy of the schools in question, subject to any general directions from the Director of Education and in consultation with the Advisory Council for African Education, and subject to directions from the supreme denominational authority in case of religious matters.

Each Board of Governors was to have a chairman nominated by denominational authority. There were to be 3 government nominees and 3 nominees of the denominational authority. The chairman and the nominated members would elect 5 members to the Board. The chairman would remain in office as long as he was wanted by the denominational authority. A third of the members would retire at end of every school year but they would be eligible for re-nomination or re-election. The headmaster would be required to present business to the Board

and to attend all its meetings although he would have no vote. The Board was required to meet at least once a year. Duties of headmaster were specified as follows:
(i) He was to be personally responsible to his Board of Governors for the academic, social and domestic organisation, and conduct of the school.
(ii) It would be his duty to arrange curriculum and syllabus as required by the Director of Education.
(iii) It would further be his duty to arrange religious instruction and education under the guidance of denominational authorities.
(iv) He was to be responsible for the feeding, medical care and welfare of pupils, and to be in charge of all employees of the Board.
(v) He was expected to make arrangements for the admission of pupils, to collect fees, to report failure to pay fees, and to report all pupils discontinued on grounds thereof.
(vi) It was his duty to furnish the parent or guardian of every pupil entering school with the statement that pupils might be expelled from school on any grounds that are considered by the Board to be in the interest of the school.
(vii) The headmaster was to furnish the Board with an annual report, cause accounts to be kept and arrange for audit of school accounts.

Inspections
The rules made self governing schools liable to inspection by panels of Education Officers. The chairman of such a panel would after inspection meet the Board of Governors to amplify the report and, after this, the report and comments on it would be submitted to the Government.

Higher Education 1922-1970
When the Directors of Education held their annual Conference in Dar-es-Salaam in March 1929, they agreed unanimously that higher education for the East Africans should be centred at Makerere, Kampala. Makerere had been in existence for at least seven years, providing higher education before any other institution. While it had started as a technical school, it had in a fairly short time embarked with considerable success on courses in Medicine, Agriculture, Elementary Engineering, Surveying, and Teacher education. Besides these professional courses, a general education programme was run which by 1935 led to the Cambridge School Certificate. From its early days, Makerere College, as it was known, was held in high esteem and the training it offered made a mark on its students.

In 1935, the Secretary of State for the Colonies appointed a Commission to examine and report on higher education in East Africa. The Commission arrived in East Africa in January 1937 with the following as members. The Right Hon. Earl de la Warr (Chairman); Mr Robert Bernays, M.P.; Miss Phillipa Esdaile, D.Sc.; Mr

B. Mowat Jones, D.S.O.; M.A., Dr Alexander Kerr, M.A., L.L.D.; Dr W. H. McLean, PH.D., M. Inst., C.E.; Mr Z. K. Matthews, M.A.., LL. B.; Dr John Murray, M. A., LL.D.; The Hon. Harold Nicholson, C.M.G., M.P.; Mr F. J. Pedler, Colonial Office (Secretary). Obviously, there was no Ugandan in the team nor was there an East African and there is no evidence to the effect that there was no such person suitable for serving on the Commission.

The Commission was asked to examine and report on the organisation and working of Makerere College and to make recommendations for its development and administration. The Commission was also to study and report on institutions or other agencies for vocational training connected with Makerere College. The educational system of the territories from which the College drew its students were to be studied and reported on. In making recommendations, the Commission was asked to consider carefully the general interest and needs of the communities from which future students might be drawn and the educational needs of the women.

The Commission carried out their mission with considerable zeal and made many long-sighted recommendations. They stressed relevance of the education programme to the environment and called for improvement and expansion of primary education - and did not forget to associate this with proper training education and better pay for primary teachers. The Commission recommended improvement of existing secondary schools and urged the Government to establish more secondary schools. The need for an East African School Leaving Examination was emphasised that should be based on a syllabus suited in content to African conditions but a standard comparable to that of examinations recognised by British Examining Bodies. The Commission wanted the education of girls to be developed as a matter of prime urgency, with stress on training for home making. The appointment of a Director of Women's Education was strongly recommended.

As far as Makerere College was directly concerned, the following specific recommendations were made:

(i) All post-secondary courses at the College and its associated institutions to form the Higher College of East Africa.
(ii) The Principal and Staff of the Higher College to be University type and to be of University status.
(iii) The Higher College should have an autonomous governing body.
(iv) The Higher College should award its own diplomas and efforts be made to secure recognition of these diplomas by Universities and professional bodies.
(v) Continuation of professional courses in Teacher Education, Medicine, Agriculture and Veterinary Science was recommended.
(vi) The Higher College to be a centre for research and to maintain contact with other research institutions.

(vii) Suitable students who completed courses at the Higher College should be encouraged to continue studies outside East Africa and the Government should state their policy regarding the employment of Africans with post-secondary education.

An international conference held in 1938 to consider the Commission's recommendations accepted in general the outline of the Higher College's structure as suggested by the Commission.

The Makerere College Ordinance of 1938 created an Asssembly for the College and the Makerere College Council. In 1938, a new Principal arrived and the use of lectures and tutorials instead of lessons and classes, the abolition of roll-calls, the prefect system and compulsory physical education were some indications (to students particularly) that Makerere had ceased to be a senior secondary school and was heading for University status.

For the next six years, 1939 - 1945, progress was slow, obviously, because of the war. However, construction of buildings went on and the main building, now the Central Administration Block, and the two chapels were ready in 1941. There was curtailment in every field and the Council endeavoured to effect strict economy of available resources. In passing, it may be mentioned that the year 1940 saw the end of the engineering course as it had become impossible to recruit staff. The number of students at the College continued to be small, standing at 181, which included 28 Kenyans, 31 Tanganyikans and 9 Zanzibarians in 1940.

The road to the status of University College (1945-60)
Despite considerable setbacks caused by the war, the Council made plans for the College to conduct academic courses which were not linked to professional training and to make provisions for the academic staff to undertake research and, wherever possible, to involve able students. To implement this, higher courses in Science and Arts were started in 1944. The Vice-Principal, Mr T. R. Batten, M. A. (Oxon), added something interesting to the curriculum. Every registered student, Science or Arts, did a one year Social Studies course which attempted to make him aware of East Africa's economic and social problems. There was also a compulsory one-year English course for all except English majors. All these courses aimed at providing a broad general background to professional training and were conducted at post School Certificate level although for some unknown reason not very many students passed the examinations at the end of the course.

In 1945, the Commission on Higher Education in the Colonies, the Asquith Commission, visiting Makerere observed and reported that in the period since the de la Warr Commission of 1937, the College had taken creditable steps towards becoming a University through the first stage of a university college. In general, their report had a favourable, positive tone and encouraged Makerere to continue in the same direction.

But Makerere could not move fast forward, although the war was over and there was a new Principal, Dr. D. Lamont, formerly Professor of Moral Philosophy, Cairo University; there were some difficult problems. To mention a few of them:

Delivery of equipment badly needed was still slow: staff recruitment presented problems as academic opportunities and scales of salary existing then were no inducement to experienced University teachers.

In spite of these difficulties, determined that the College should develop further, the East African High Commission (the three Governors) assented to the Makerere College Act on 24 February 1949. The Act made provision for government control and administration of Makerere College. Under the Act, a Council of 14 members under the chairmanship of Sir R. E. Robins, C.M.G., O.B.E., was set up. Suprisingly, there was no African on it and there can be no acceptable explanation for this omission as there were a few eligible Africans.

Soon after the Makerere College Act, the Inter-University Council dispatched delegates to conduct on the spot discussions on the future development of the College. The delegates, five in number and all of them experienced University teachers and administrators, together with the Makerere Academic Board, after long discussions, came out with a plan, subject to the approval of London University, to enable students to read for external degrees of the University of London. London University accepted the proposals and degree courses started in March 1950. The delegates and Makerere lecturers suggested that, for the time being, the requirements for admission to the degree course would be a pass in a test of competence in English Language plus a number of credits at School Certificate Examinations. The first two years (equivalent of A-level) would be spent preparing student candidates for London University Intermediate Examinations.

The intermediate course started in March 1950 with a group that not only had passed the College entrance examination but also had passed Cambridge School Certificate Examinations. In this first lot, was a woman student who, having passed School Certificate Exams, was admitted to a Science course and later became the first woman to qualify as medical doctor at Makerere. Makerere became the University College of East Africa. It had professional schools of Agriculture, Medicine, Veterinary Science, Education. Faculties of Science and Arts and a School of Fine Art. There were about 200 Students.

When the University College started preparing students for London University external degrees in science and arts, there was the problem of professional schools which were not covered by the special relation with London University terms. There was, for example, no provision for these professional schools to prepare their students for external degrees of London University in Medicine or Agriculture. Teachers in the Faculty of Science had the dis-spiriting experience of having spent two years getting a promising student through the intermediate examination and, when he was ready for entry to a degree course, he would be lost to a professional school. Those who entered professional schools ended with professional diplomas, not degrees. The Medical School particularly raised its standards and awarded a qualification, the licentiate in Medicine and Surgery (E.A.), which entitled its holder to registration as a medical practitioner in East Africa. This qualification was recognised by the General Medical Council of Great Britain in 1958. In the same year, the degrees of B.Sc. (Agric) and B.Sc. (Econ.) were introduced.

In 1961, the University College of East Africa became Makerere University College. After that, in response to the country's manpower requirements and as a result of the expansion of advanced-level work at Secondary Schools, the University College grew considerably in numbers of students, teachers, facilities, and variety of courses.

On 1 July 1970, Makerere University College, for about nine years a constituent College of the University of East Africa, became a full fledged University and was named Makerere University, Kampala. Every effort has been made since then to provide more and more facilities at Makerere for programmes to meet Uganda's manpower needs and requirements. The numbers of students and staff have shot up and the University continues to enjoy the prestige, in respect of standards, that it has always enjoyed and remains the prized goal of all Ugandans aspiring to higher education. Two new faculties, Technology and Veterinary Science, have been started and the construction of their facilities is under way at the time of writing this account 1971.

Education 1945 - 62

The first six years of this period were, generally speaking, a difficult time for education. According to a 10 year development plan drawn up by Dr E. B. Worthington (the author of Science in Africa) in this period emphasis was to be placed on increasing economic production and not on improving social services. However, the new Governor, Sir Andrew Benjamin Cohen (1952 - 1956), having stressed that economic expansion would be impossible unless accompanied by social and political advancement, appointed a Committee under the chairmanship of Mr B. de Bunsen, Principal of Makerere College, to investigate and report on the state of education and submit proposals for the future organisation and development of education in Uganda. The de Bunsen Committee made three important recommendations:

(i) That there should be a vigorous reorganisation of the Teacher Training System, involving the raising of entrance qualifications and a reduction in the number of Teacher's Colleges from 41 to 23 for efficiency.
(ii) That the Senior Secondary course be of four year duration after an eight year primary course.
(iii) That Local Education Authorities, i.e. District Councils be responsible for primary education.

The Committee also studied teacher's conditions of service and recommended new pay scales. This had been long overdue; all over the country teachers were unhappy about what they were paid for the heavy duties they shouldered.

The Government accepted and put into effect the Committee's recommendations; indeed, the proposals made by the de Bunsen committee provided the guidelines for educational expansion for ten years.

It was also in the period under review that the Education Ordinance 1959 was enacted. The most important aspect of the Ordinance was that under its section 33, the Board of Governors (Self Governing Schools) Rules were promulgated and published in 1962 and have been in operation to date. Briefly, the rules required, after their publication, that for every school there shall be a Board of Governors consisting of:

(i) A Chairman appointed by the body that had founded the school (e.g. Church or Government) with the approval of the Minister of Education.
(ii) Eight nominated members approved by the Minister, four of whom should be nominated by the foundation body and four nominated by the Chief Education Officer.
(iii) Four members elected by the Chairman and nominated members but approved by the Minister.
(iv) A Secretary appointed by the Board.

One of the tasks assigned to the Board in the Rules has been exercising supervisory control of the headmaster, teaching staff and non-teaching staff as agreed between the Board and the foundation body. The Rules also spelled out in greater detail the duties of the headmaster. With the commencement of these Rules the Self-Governing (Grant-in-Aid) Rules 1943 and School Management Administrative Instructions were revoked.

Education since 1962

The Government of independent Uganda takes positive steps to control and administer education effectively.

In January 1963, a Commission under the chairmanship of Professor E. B. Castle, formerly Professor of Education, Hull University, was appointed to report on education in Uganda with the following terms of reference:

To examine in the light of the approved recommendations of the International Bank Survey Mission Report and Uganda's financial position and future manpower requirements, the content and structure of education in Uganda; to consider how it may be improved and adapted to the needs of this country and to submit recommendations accordingly.

The Commission which had the services of a number of outstanding Ugandan men of learning, addressed themselves with considerable skill to the exacting task of visualising the needs of an independent state and recommending a school structure to meet these needs.

The Commission made the following main recommendations:
(i) Primary course to last seven years instead of eight.
(ii) A revision of the primary syllabus to be undertaken so as to produce pupils better prepared for life and future study than hitherto.

(iii) That there should be established four types of post primary institutions to admit a proportion of primary school leavers.
(a) High Schools-offering an academic course although some of them could have a technical bias.
(b) Secondary Schools-to offer general and vocational education.
(c) Technical Schools-to conduct a four year course leading to City Guilds Examinations.
(d) Farm Schools-to conduct a four year course.

Government education policy after the Castle Report.
The Publication of the Castle Report was followed by the publication of Government's Sessional Paper No. 4 of 1963 in which the Government set out its policy on the report in particular and in general. At the same time the Education (Amendment) Act 1963 was enacted to enable the Central Government, as it was called then, to secure sufficient control over all details of educational planning and development throughout the country.

The debate on responsibility and control.
The Castle Report assigned the responsibility for education in Uganda to the Central and Local Governments. However, on the question of control, only three of the members of the Commission expressed the view that this should belong to the Central and Local Governments, too. It seemed, thus, by implication that the control and supervision of schools was believed by the majority of the commissioners to belong to voluntary agencies. In one of the longest debates on education in Parliament here, the Government made it absolutely clear that the voluntary agencies would thenceforward not control schools. The Government was going to control schools.

Up to 1963, some post-primary institutions, secondary schools, teacher training colleges, technical schools and, except for a very small number of Primary schools in urban areas, the greatest number of primary schools were administered and managed on a religious denominational basis by voluntary agencies. The voluntary agencies were Catholic Missions, the Uganda Muslim Education Association and Protestant Missions.

It is true there was a number of inter-denominational primary schools founded by the Local and Central Governments just as there were inter-denominational secondary schools again founded by the Central Government, but we think it is safe to say that their number was small. Each of the three voluntary agencies had an educational secretary general with his headquarters in Kampala. Under each educational secretary general, each voluntary agency had an education secretary in charge of junior secondary schools and, wherever possible, for each district or for every two districts, a school supervisor with several assistants and auxiliary clerical and accountancy staff. With this administrative set-up, the voluntary agencies had a considerable amount of control in the schools, particularly to the extent that they decided who should be admitted, who should teach there and who should be headmaster. It was, under the system as it existed, unthinkable for a Catholic to head a Protestant school or for a Moslem to head any of the Christian voluntary agencies' schools. For many years there had been intensive rivalry among voluntary agencies in setting up schools in many parts of the country. Except for a few foundations which trace their beginnings back to the early 1920's, for example, Kibuli School, the Uganda Muslim Education Association had come late into the field of setting up schools, but was doing well by 1963. The Muslim agency had many schools though not as many as each of the other agencies had.

The system was particularly wasteful of the country's limited resources; for instance, the use of three supervisors in an area where one supervisor would have been adequate; or half empty schools simply because there were not enough pupils of the faith which the voluntary agency represented. It was not unusual for a pupil to walk past a school near his/her home to a distant school because that was the institution managed by his denomination (where he would be accepted because of the faith of his parents).

In 1964, the Government abolished the posts of education secretary general, education secretaries and school supervisors; after this, all matters concerning primary and junior secondary schools were centralised in Area Education Offices. Except in Buganda where the then Kabaka's Government obliquely controlled some secondary schools till 1966, all secondary schools in the country came under the direct control of Central Government in 1964.

To implement the changes, firstly, at least 54 Assistant Education Officers were appointed for work in Area Education Offices. Secondly, the Chief Education Officer was given powers to require a teacher to serve in any school in Uganda and to retire teachers.

The implementation of the reorganisation of administration and control of schools was not accepted without some resistance. One of the main arguments put forward by the leaders of the resistance, where it occurred, was that ownership of the school buildings (voluntary agencies claimed ownership of school buildings) could not be separated from the administration and control of the schools. Resistance in some part, therefore, though unsuccessful, appeared in the form of Missions threatening to withdraw buildings from being used for school purposes under the new policy although this was usually settled amicably sooner or later.

Since the Castle Report was published, remarkable progress has been made. First of all, the integration of the separate racial and religious systems, which were a main feature of education before 1962, has now been completed.

A child can gain admission to any school irrespective of his race or religion and without fear that he will be compelled to undergo religious instructions in order to keep his place in the school. Secondly, there has been an expansion in facilities for secondary education to an extent unheard of and never even expected before independence. As a result, many girls and boys have been offered the opportunity of secondary education. The tables given below show the magnitude of the numbers of those who have benefited from secondary education at aided schools in the period 1963 - 1968:

Year	Intake S1.	Total output S4.	Total enrolment S1-4
1963	3067	1907	9,542
1964	4100	2068	11,709
1965	6106	2499	16,192
1966	6504	3029	20,003
1967	8468	4239	25,180
1968	9085	5936	30,026

Higher School Certificate:

Year	Intake S5.	Total output S6.	Total enrolment S5 - 6
1963	399	254	653
1964	575	368	943
1965	608	523	1,131
1966	966	579	1,545
1967	941	904	1,845
1968	1,290	932	2,222

The figures in the above tables do not include the numbers of pupils in what are known as private schools, of which there are many.

Finally, technical education has received more attention than the period before 1963. The Uganda Technical College, the apex of technical education here, until 1967 accepted students for undergraduate level engineering courses which were completed at Srathclyde University in Scotland; they were suspended in 1968. For active technician preparation was being made to start degree-level work in engineering at Makerere. Technician and craft courses have continued, however, and with the assistance of a team of UNESCO specialists, the College has trained a good number of engineering technicians. At the same time, some of the Uganda lecturers have been given fellowships for further study overseas in the United Kingdom so that they can take over from the UNESCO team.

By the end of 1967, there were five Technical Schools with an enrolment of 1,177 students in the following courses: Boat Building, Block Laying and Concrete Practice, Carpentry and Joinery, Electrical Installations, Machine Shop

Engineering, Motor Vehicle Mechanics, Painting and Decorating, Plumbing, and Gin-fitting. All these, obviously, are very useful courses for making available technicians with skills often called for in many areas of activity.

At the time of writing, proposals have reached an advanced form for raising the standards of entry into technical institutions, updating the courses they offer, and for the Uganda Technical College to play an even bigger role in producing more and more men with technical know-how to meet the manpower requirements that have been thrust on the country by the technological age we live in.

In the period under review, the Uganda College of Commerce has been established to help students who have already reached a good general academic education to prepare for careers in commerce. It has attracted many students leaving secondary schools, and, its newly established Department of Distribution, which gives comprehensive training to Ugandans intending to set up in business, is a very important part of the College now.

PART TWO

THE TASK AND CHALLENGE OF THE DEVELOPMENT OF TEACHER EDUCATION

2

Teacher Education to 1925 and after

Teachers in traditional Uganda

Before the coming of the missionaries to Uganda, (followed by the British colonial administrators, during the latter part of the nineteenth century), if boys and girls grew up to maturity lacking in the knowledge of essential skills, customs, and social deportment within a particular community, their parents were blamed for having failed in their duty to educate them. By implication, this would mean that before the establishment of schools in Uganda on the basis of Western education, there were no professional teachers in the sense we know them today. But that parents mainly shouldered the responsibility of teaching their children. While they did this job, society also joined in to help them, especially where manners and social values and interaction with other people were concerned. Any adult person within a particular community was responsible for condemning wrong social attitudes and behaviours and for showing the right thing to the young. This was his/her responsibility as a member of the community, even if the young person in question was not one of his/her children. The propagation and custody of the social values of the group meant the strengthening of that particular society and ensured that it stayed strong and ready to withstand any onslaught that might lead to destruction by the forces of other groups of people who had different values. This safeguarding of the social values of a group meant also order and stability within that single group of people; so it was the duty of every member to follow those values and to demonstrate them to the young.

There were also what one could call professional teachers. These were men and women who possessed rare technical skills and medical knowledge within each group of people who taught these essentials to some of the young. These rare skills and medical lore did not need to be possessed by every one in the society. So, a skilled iron smith, a skilled potter, a knowledgeable medicine man or woman, a skilled canoe maker, and men and women in the families of chiefs and kings connected with the political administration of the group taught not only their children the knowledge connected with these skills but also other children who were sent to them to be brought up with such skills and knowledge.

On the introduction of school education, as opposed to the education whereby the 'homestead was the school, the fire-place the classroom and everywhere human activity took place was the laboratory', the three categories of teachers were gradually pushed into the background. First of all, in the new order, the content of education was imparted to pupils differently. While the above three groups of teachers, mentioned earlier in this account, could teach the young about how their group had travelled from afar to occupy that area they were settled in then; and the reasons for having left the original land; while they taught about their leaders and the battles fought and won, or lost; and why all that was the subject of history - the missionaries, on the other hand, taught how the Vikings had invaded Britain from the north of Europe; how Hannibal of Carthage had lost his eye fighting with the Romans, crossing the Alps on elephants to do so; and how the Europeans had invaded America and overpowered the natives there. The Uganda teacher of the pre-Colonial era had taught the young about the lie of the land, the flora and fauna of their areas, the lakes and the flow of the rivers and the different seasons of the year. For this was their geography. The missionaries, however, began to teach about the Thames and the English Channel, the American Mississippi and the Asian Ganges, and how gigantic trees grew and were felled in Canada and then rolled down the river; and they also taught them the four fantastic European and American seasons. Indeed, besides the above subjects, the missionaries taught reading and writing, entirely new skills that were really a new wonder. One could go on and mention something about other subjects taught by the Africans before the arrival of the missionaries but which were to be approached from a different angle and were given Anglo-Saxon names such as history, geography, arithmetic, religion, nature study and hygiene. But, the point which we want to stress here is that both the content and the names of subjects lay outside the African context. Consequently the three already mentioned categories of African teachers were technically knocked out from the teaching profession.

Unfortunately, those young people who started to attend the lessons of the missionaries were given the impression by their teachers that education means strictly what the missionaries were talking about in what came to be called schools and not what the elders helplessly continued to talk about around the fire place and in the homestead. This teaching began to be regarded by the young as nothing more than interesting stories to while away time, especially at night, and to be gradually disregarded and given less attention by them. After all, it never formed even part of the answers which they had to produce, either oral or written, when the missionaries set them tests to ascertain how much they had got out of education or to give them certificates to pass out of school and go into the world as 'educated' men and women. The number of the young who came to enjoy the new kind of education grew slowly, in fact, by the time formal schools began to be established in Uganda (from roughly 1898), the three categories of native teachers continued to teach the young, especially those who did not join the new schools. But their influence was on the losing side as parents gradually started to realise that if their children were to rise in the new order and struggle on equal terms for advantages with those children who were joining the new schools, they too had to send their children to the missionary schools. Thus, the increase of children going to listen to the teaching of the Mission meant that the work became too much for the missionaries. To cope with it, they decided to start educating a new kind of African teacher who would help them in the school work.

Missionaries train teachers to assist them

The sheer impossibility of a few missionaries coping with the religious and secular education work for the whole of Uganda necessitated from the very beginning the coaching of some of the more promising Ugandans in the art of transmitting the new content of education to their fellow Africans to aid the missionaries. The determination of the missionaries, both Roman Catholic and Protestant, was to spread churches and schools in the whole of Uganda as fast as possible. Indeed, their primary aim was to spread the word of God using the tenets of the Bible. But the planting of this doctrine about God had to go hand in hand with the founding of schools that would have, as their primary aim, the spread of secular knowledge connected with Christian principles. So, the establishment of a church building served as a school on week days to teach both Christianity and secular knowledge, and as a place of worship on Sunday and on holy days. These small church-cum-schools began to be manned by African teachers as we shall see below.

The missionaries would choose the most brilliant and promising boys and get them to help teach the slow learners, or those who had just joined the mission school. The more brilliant, let us say, or the more enthusiastic boys would easily show themselves; it was about such that Bishop Alfred Tucker, Bishop of Uganda wrote in 1898:

> 'No sooner was one piece of writing taught to them than they clamoured for another one. It was a pleasure to see that once a boy or man who had been a faithful listener at the foot of the missionary an hour ago, in the next hour had a group of eager listeners surrounding him while he was trying to teach them the written piece taught to him by the missionary'.

Many of these young men sprang up and they were gradually given some coaching in passing on knowledge to others. As they became proficient, they would either be left at the post where the missionaries would help them or they would be sent to pioneer new outpost stations where they would start smaller schools, primarily meant to teach religion with a sprinkling of reading and writing. Such a school was called a catechist's school. The same man managed a small church where on Sundays he led prayers, read the Gospel, stressed the moral of the Gospel, read and tried to apply it to the general behaviour of the people. He would then finally tell the faithful what the European missionary wanted them to do and perhaps inform them of the day he would visit the place.

The above was the first way of getting teachers. As education in the Mission post progressed higher, that is when classes of a Mission school increased from primary one to primary six during the first decade of the twentieth century, a second group of African teachers also began to emerge. If those boys, and to a small extent girls, showed exceptional ability at studies, completed primary four or six and wanted to teach, they would be coached so as to teach predominantly secular subjects, though with Christian doctrine as the basis. The period of their preparation as teachers ranged from one year to two years, usually depending on the speed at which they mastered the pedagogical skills. Then, they would be entrusted with their own classes, normally, teaching primary one to three and leaving the higher classes to the missionaries. They were also entrusted to found sub-grade schools consisting of one or two primary classes away from the main Mission post where again a church would be part of the establishment. These schools were usually referred to as 'the school in the bush' to differentiate them from those schools which were at the Mission post where the missionaries stayed. A mission school would have a number of such sub-grade schools which would be treated as its feeder schools.

Generally, the catechist who managed the village church, sometimes near a sub-grade school, was the man who had not gone high enough in academic matters. Usually, he had only been confirmed in the church, learnt the art of reading and writing very well, and was knowledgeable about the Bible and in the catechism of his denomination. At times he might have attended primary one and then decided to become a partner of the missionary in the spreading of the word of God. Normally he was a man who was devout and bent on being an exemplary person in the Christian faith before his neighbours. He taught his pupils primarily the catechism and some reading and writing. Some of these pupils would have been baptised as infants while others were preparing themselves to be baptised as adult Christians. After staying two or three years with the catechist, they would be taken to the Mission where they would complete their education in the confirmation of the faith either according to the Roman Catholic or the Protestant way. Then, after this process, those who had parents who were able to send them to primary schools would either join primary one of the Mission school or primary one of the sub-grade school, depending generally on which of them was nearer their home. If a pupil managed to complete the sub-grade school and wanted to go on with learning, he would go and join the Mission primary school starting with primary three.

In this way, a number of out-post sub-grade schools grew up and out-post sub-churches managed by a new kind of African teacher fed the main Mission post. These two kinds of teachers played a very important role in helping to spread both secular and Christian education far and wide in the country side. Both groups of teachers, either teaching at the Mission post with the missionaries or teaching away from it in the villages, were deeply religious and were under an obligation to their missionary masters to display by precept and example the Christian behaviour in their areas. They had to attend Sunday services and play a leading role in the services, either by presiding over prayers or Christian hymns. Failure to exemplify Christian behaviour to both faithful and non-faithful (the so-called pagans) meant dismissal. For example, they were required to have one wife, to restrain their social enjoyment and to have homes that would be copied by their neighbours. Of course, all these restrictions were applied to any one Christian but to a teacher they were applied without any possibility of relaxation.

By 1920 certain Mission posts had been earmarked as special places where those students who were intending to be teachers had to spend a year or two being coached while helping in teaching. So, not every missionary could coach his own teachers at his primary school. The first way of bringing up teachers had been seen to be rather haphazard. In the new special Mission posts an attempt was made to provide missionary tutors who knew more about how a teacher should best be brought up; teaching materials were gathered in such 'teacher training' Missions in order to provide a more effective education for the teachers. The catechists, however, continued to be recruited and initiated in every Mission post by the missionaries who were in charge of the Mission post as their job did not need much preparation. They were only called back every month to the Mission post to be given more hints as to how they could better their work.

Government influence and participation in teacher education

After the establishment of the Education Department and the appointment of the Director of Education in 1925, as already mentioned, the Government began to take an interest in the training of teachers. One of the main requirements of the Department of Education was that each missionary group should establish formal teacher training schools with qualified staff to train Primary School teachers. There was no need to talk about African teachers for Secondary Schools since such schools did not begin to operate seriously until the 1930s, and even when they did, they were staffed by Europeans. Each missionary society responded by setting up Teachers' Schools, or Normal Schools, as they were often then referred to. Teachers' Schools served linguistic areas as the teachers were to teach predominantly in the vernacular of given areas.

To enumerate the centres that were set up then would make a long list which is unnecessary since nearly every year new centres sprang up whenever a demand arose due to the progressively increasing number of pupils joining Primary Schools every year.

Makerere College, a Government foundation begins training teachers

Makerere College began running a teacher's course in 1925. It started by calling on twenty-five serving and competent teachers, trained them for three years, and sent them out to teach in classes that would be the equivalent of present day P6 and P7 which up to then had been reserved for the missionaries.

It was this teacher's course which gave birth to the now prominent school of Education at Makerere University Kampala. By 1929 students began to come from the rest of East Africa to Makerere to attend the course. About 1930 the Government, through the Education Department, ran a Teachers' School at Nyanjeeradde on top of Makerere hill to train teachers from all over the country who would use Kiswahili as a medium of instruction in the Primary Schools. But the life of the teacher's school at Nyanjeeradde was short because the Government had no primary schools of its own to which to post its Nyanjeeradde teachers. The missionaries were not too happy to see the Government set up its own teacher's schools. There was a feeling that Nyanjeeradde teachers were not likely to be responsive to missionary direction. Moreover, the missionaries and chiefs were not in favour of introducing Kiswahili in Uganda for fear that its use would kill the local vernacular languages. And as we saw in chapter one, missionaries who had written books in Luganda, for instance, argued fiercely against the introduction of Kiswahili here. The Government Normal School at Nyanjeeradde was transferred to Kasawo about 30 miles north east of Kampala to serve as a teacher training school for Muslim boys. Early in 1950 it was again transferred to Kibuli.

During the 1940s the education of the teacher underwent a change in order to raise educational standards in, the whole educational system of the country. The students joining the teachers colleges before 1940 were in two categories. The first category was joining what were vernacular teacher training centres. Such students had completed primary four and a few exceptional ones had not gone that far in academic attainment - they had been teachers in sub-grade schools and had either completed primary two or three but had shown that they were intelligent young men and women; so they had been recommended by both the missionaries and the inspectors of schools to join a teachers' college to get a teaching certificate. Both these and the above group would have a course lasting for three years and after the course they would teach primary one to four. They were called vernacular teachers because they were supposed to teach in vernacular languages.

The second category of teachers was that of men, and a few women who were attending a teachers' course at Makerere College for three years after their Junior Secondary School education, that is nine years of education. These, on completing the course, went to teach primary five and six. It was out of this group of people that a few African headmasters for some primary schools were appointed; the missionaries tended to head most of the schools before the 1940s. By 1939 the standard of entry to teachers' courses at Makerere College was raised and aspiring students had to join the course after finishing class twelve at a secondary school; on completion of training they were supposed to teach in the junior secondary section, that is the three classes above primary six.

It thus became necessary to train another category of teachers to teach in primary five and six where Makerere trained teachers had been teaching. In the early 1940s teacher training centres recruited and trained students with junior secondary qualification for three years at the end of which they came out as primary teachers.

At the same time, by 1940 it was felt that students with primary four qualification were too low in academic attainment to teach. So it was decided by the Department of Education to raise the entry qualification of students entering vernacular teacher training schools. In future, such students would have to have a primary leaving certificate, obtained after primary six. Yet they would continue to teach in the vernacular from primary one to four.

The most promising teachers of those who had got their qualifications earlier after completing primary four would gradually be retained to reach the new standard of those few whose entry into the teachers' colleges had been raised to primary six. The rest would continue teaching still, but be given continual refresher courses until they would eventually retire. There was quite a large number of these teachers; some of whom were up-graded and others who were not up-graded; they continued teaching up to the early 1950s. This had an adverse effect, however, on the standards of pupils. While some of the old type could be up-graded, it did not mean that they really attained the same standards academically as the new type. Sometimes the situation had also changed in the schools. In particular, they had been used to handling fewer pupils in classes of about fifteen to twenty-five. Now they had to cope with classes of forty pupils and more because the 1940s saw a great increase in the number of pupils being enrolled in primary schools. That was because parents had realised beyond any doubt that if their children had to get opportunities in future they had to send them to school. Text books had also changed slightly and so had the syllabus; one can imagine the problems which they had to struggle with and try to surmount.

In response to the recommendations of the de Bunsen Education Committee of 1953, small uneconomic teacher training colleges had to be phased out and finally closed down. Denominational groups, the Native Anglican Church (now the Church of Uganda) and the Roman Catholic Mission, had established teacher training colleges in many parts of the country for members of their denominations. Generally, these colleges were not far apart in distance. They could even be just three or four kilometers apart. The majority of these primary teacher training colleges, particularly teachers of P1 to P4, were small. For one thing, they were sited in such a way as to serve a particular linguistic group of Uganda peoples, because instruction had to be in a language locally used which might be quite strange to students from other parts of the country.

The practice of operating colleges on a denominational basis, plus the fact that the colleges were sited in particular areas, made the establishment and development of large teacher training colleges to take large numbers of students from a wide area impossible. Many of these small colleges which existed then were, to say the least, expensive to run, inefficient and hardly up to the required standard. In the first place, it was difficult to get qualified staff for each of them. The ones that managed to get qualified and specialised staff could not fully utilise them as the number of students was much below the optimum. Some colleges found it hard to obtain adequate teaching materials. Those that had materials found they were underused. Secondly, as already mentioned, the small colleges were expensive to run. Each establishment had to maintain its own staff and Principal and had to pay these people salaries - although they were only teaching a small number of students.

The de Bunsen Committee justifiably recommended their numerical reduction and the building/development of large ones, though still on denominational lines. The language problem would not arise as it was proposed that after 1952 students joining teacher training would have completed primary 8 or junior secondary 2 successfully and, therefore, they could be taught in English. By 1960 the number of primary teachers' colleges had been reduced from about 55 to 22. It had been planned after 1965 to absorb all the existing primary teachers' colleges into four massive regional teachers' colleges built in four carefully selected places. But, so far, it has not been possible to do this and the idea has been abandoned. Instead, it was planned to expand 10 of the existing 20 Teachers' colleges in the period 1974 - 80 so that each could initially take 135 students but later on raise the enrolment to 500 students. The colleges marked for expansion were Ngetta, Kinyamasika, Ibanda, Busubizi, Ndejje, Nkozi, Kabwangasi, Nyondo (men), Nyondo (women). Furthermore, it was planned to put up and operate 10 entirely new colleges in selected places.

It should be noted that the de Bunsen Committee recommended a thoroughgoing raising of the standard of all teachers' colleges so that they might produce teachers who could effectively teach in the type of primary schools envisaged for the 1950s and 1960s.

The problem of new syllabuses, use of English as medium of instruction, and the old-type of primary teacher

Many of the teachers who had undergone teacher-training after six years of formal education posed a problem; it seemed as if the use of English as the medium of instruction plus the use of new syllabuses would make them redundant. As their services were still required, it was arranged to put them through refresher and up-grading courses at which a reasonable number did well and for some years kept teaching up to the 4th form of the Primary Schools. But by the early 1960s the bulk of these then called vernacular teachers had been delegated to teach in primary 1 and primary 2. It ought to be pointed out that this was unfortunate because at this time the age of pupils in these lower forms was such that they needed to be taught by people who had been trained in the use of infant methods of teaching and, as far as we know, vernacular teachers had not had this in their training. In 1954 training of vernacular teachers was discontinued.

The rise of grade 3 teachers

Up to 1947, Junior Secondary (currently known as P7 and P8 and one more class) classes were taught by Makerere College trained teachers and expatriate missionary teachers. This section of the school system was meant to prepare selected pupils for three more years after primary education. Developments which had started at Makerere in 1941 indicated particularly clearly that it would not be long before the College stopped producing the Junior Secondary teachers or, if it continued, in sufficient numbers. In 1946, therefore, Junior Secondary teachers' courses were started at Buloba, Namagunga, and Kisubi- and at Mbarara by the Government in 1948. By the Independence date 1962, only the Government founded College, formerly at Mbarara but then situated at Kyambogo near Kampala, conducted grade 3 teacher training courses. With the abolition of Junior Secondary classes, grade 3 teachers became staff for the upper forms of the primary school.

3

Training of teachers for Secondary Schools ups and downs, 1953 - 1970

Why train the teachers?
The main point to discuss is whether we need to train and engage people as certified teachers. There is a certain amount of feeling among many citizens of Uganda that the teaching profession is not strictly a profession. Such people feel that teaching children can be done by anybody, trained or untrained, so long as such a person has been to school. This point of view arises from erroneous ideas about the duties of a teacher within a school and within the whole education system of the country. Such people look at these two aspects of a teacher's role and think that there is no more to them, than to stand up in front of a class of eager boys and girls near a chalk board with chalk in hand, white or coloured, and talk, then give written tests, mark them, and then promote pupils to the next class or retain them in one class. The problem is more complex than this. And, if we continue to think of teaching in this narrow sense, so much the worse for our hopes of progress. We shall continue to have people teaching our young children who have not the breadth of vision to understand the totality of what the teaching profession means and entails.

To belong to the teaching profession calls for the variety of skills for which a person needs to have been prepared at least or brought into a situation where he / she can see how they work. One has got to learn about methods of transmitting knowledge in the most convenient and coherent manner so that the learners can learn easily and resourcefully. If people just leave school at whatever level and plunge into teaching without any meaningful initiation, this kind of approach will be lacking in the way they teach. They will be more concerned with pouring out facts for pupils to cram, without any reference to the true end result - that of producing educated persons; persons who will use what they have learned to acquire an approach to their life which may never need those facts, but which can deal with all kinds of situations.

Secondly, belonging to a teaching profession means that a person is called upon to plan a meaningful scheme of work for the class in different subjects, so as to see how it fits in with the totality of a school curriculum and the ideals of our Republic. An untrained teacher does not see beyond the mere facts that he / she gives to the children and he / she is unable to plan these mysteries.

Thirdly, belonging to the teaching profession means that a person may be called upon to take part in research into the educational problems of our Republic, and devise suggestions for changing the curriculum so as to achieve our ideals better, using our schools. Then there is the job of preparing and testing teaching materials and then producing them. All this belongs to the realm of a professionally trained teacher. Any one would wonder how on earth an untrained person could do them satisfactorily.

Fourthly, a professionally trained teacher will be called upon to take part in the administration, supervision and planning of the whole educational system of Uganda. This is an intricate problem and if some people feel that we should leave it to anybody who has not been exposed academically to its problems, we are only being unrealistic, if not naïve.

Then we need to have people, who, because they have been brought up professionally as teachers, can make it their practice to think in terms of their profession. They can engage in meaningful professional discussions about the educational system and about their job. It is in this way that there grows an informed professional group of people who are ever alert to the problems of their job. Untrained people are not capable of this; they look at the problem of education only as their job which is to stand before a class of pupils and talk and write on the chalk board and give tests, the framing of which may be entirely meaningless, and then go back home, having finished their daily obligation. If the teaching profession is to be dominated by such people, our educational system will lack resourcefulness and will be characterised by lack of imagination. It will be in shambles.

Degree courses for teachers
When Makerere College began to grant degrees to students in 1953, the Faculty of Education extended its diploma course to postgraduate students who wanted to teach. Whereas the first group of students with Higher School Certificate level of general education spent two years training, the post graduate students spent one year. The first group continued to be allocated for teaching to the first two classes of Senior Secondary section which, from 1956, was run on the basis of four years instead of three years, according to the de Bunsen reorganisation of the educational system. The graduates were supposed to teach in any class of the Senior Secondary section. But their number grew very slowly because for jobs in Government and in the private sector, they were offered better salaries and better conditions of service than the teaching profession could offer them. Also, one had to lose a year without getting a salary while one was doing a diploma course in education. Thus, the teaching profession was not so attractive to the graduate. In an attempt to attract postgraduate students to join teaching, in 1960, Professor E. Lucas, then head of the Faculty of Education, persuaded the

Government to pay salaries to graduates for one academic year while they were on the postgraduate course in education. The government agreed to this proposal. As a result, a few more graduates were attracted to the course. Yet it was still just a trickle so that by 1962 there were only 25 graduate teachers because, once again, other occupations offered better terms of service and a greater chance of promotion, more quickly than the teaching profession. A headship seemed to be the only promotional post yet most of these were held by expatriates. Some people had the impression that the administration did not regard an African graduate teacher as fit to head a secondary school of about six hundred boys and girls. Yet an African could make a Minister. There was an acute shortage of African graduate teachers. To remedy this, government officials often visited Britain and the United States to recruit graduate teachers. These teachers were paid higher salaries and given the best houses because, it was claimed, they had been induced to come and serve in a foreign country under adverse conditions.

The Diploma course for non-graduates is transferred to Kyambogo
Further development in teacher education came in 1963 when the diploma course for non-graduates was phased out at Makerere and transferred to the National Teachers College, Kyambogo. The Faculty of Education continued to run the diploma course for one year for the post-graduate students; at the same time, the Faculty initiated a teachers degree course under the name of the Bachelor of Education which would be pursued academically for three years. The degree course, however, was phased out in 1972 because the Ministry of Education felt that, while the content of the course included a lot of education, it only allowed students to pursue one subject to degree level. It was felt that it was necessary to get teachers who had carried two subjects to degree level as it would be more viable to employ them in Secondary Schools - either teaching the two subjects in the Secondary School section of their particular schools or by easily teaching one or the other subject as need demanded in the whole secondary section. The Bachelor of Education degree course has been replaced by another one whereby students study two subjects either in Science or Arts Faculties. To do this well the Faculty of Education keeps a four term year. Students undergoing this training graduate with both a degree and a diploma in education within three years and go straight to teach in our Secondary Schools.

The diploma for the postgraduate students, however, continues to run for those who decide to become teachers after getting their degrees. Fortunately, more and more graduates are now joining this course and, this is glad news to all those Ugandans who desire to see that their schools are filled by young men and women of this country.

Both the Bachelor of Education degree course and the present course which replaced it were devised to produce graduate teachers in large numbers and rapidly. The Bachelor of Education course during its short life of nine years proved popular and it managed to produce 410 graduate teachers. But the course which replaced it was devised to produce graduate teachers in larger numbers and in a short time. The course which replaced it may prove in due course to be even more popular. Already, within two years of its inception, the course has 450 enrolled students. Of course, this is partly due to the fact that students now realise that with diminishing employment opportunities on graduation, it is the teaching profession which still offers relatively unlimited chances of employment which is definite and secure. There is also some nationalistic feeling, though perhaps not explicit in the minds of these young men and women, a desire to see that the teaching profession which is meant to shape the minds of the young towards feelings of loyalty to our country is not dominated by expatriates.

The diploma course at Kyambogo

The other device for beating the shortage of Secondary School teachers was the running of a diploma course for non-graduates at the National Teachers College Kyambogo, starting in 1964, the diploma being granted by Makerere University. But if this diploma course continues, it is likely to breed certain undesirable consequences in our educational system. First of all, the graduates of this teachers' college are vaguely supposed to teach in the lower forms of the Secondary Section, though indeed some are found teaching quite competently even up to secondary four, depending on the shortage of teachers in a particular school. The level of their academic attainment certainly allows them to teach competently up to secondary four. But research has shown that where they are paired with graduate teachers they are accepted reluctantly by the pupils whom they teach who erroneously feel that they should be taught only by teachers with degrees. The fact is that the students in secondary five and six might not accept them if the headmaster of a particular Secondary School ran short of graduate staff and were to push one of them on to these students.

Secondly, the holders of this diploma do not feel secure and easy in a school where they are paired with graduate teachers who, as academic arrogance the world over some times unfortunately dictates, treat them not quite as their equals, and are likely to delegate to them responsibilities of an inferior nature and even give them less attractive houses in a school. So professional relations are not all that smooth.

Thirdly, to safeguard themselves, they naturally seek opportunities to get entry to Makerere University or to another university through a government bursary or scholarship. A few lucky ones manage to get one of these grants and continue their studies to get degrees. This practice has the implication that the government pays twice for such people's education where it could easily cut down this expense if our educational system offered the degree courses straight to them. But as we shall see later the standards of entry to the degree course for teachers must be high.

Fourthly, this diploma course has outlived its usefulness and if it were stopped, our teaching profession would be saved from embarrassment in future. If the Faculty of Education at Makerere continues to enroll students at its present rate every year and reaches the stipulated number of 500 a year, both undergraduates and graduates, in five years' time we shall have 2,500 graduate teachers in the field, and, if you take the present 569 already in the field, we shall have nearly 3069 of them in all (of course, with a small allowance of a few teachers who will have left the profession to join other activities or through other exigencies). In five year' time the present number of Government Secondary Schools may grow from the present 75 to 80, and if each school is to have a pick of 30 graduate teachers, these schools will have 2,400 graduate teachers with 669 qualified graduate teachers waiting to be employed (perhaps this number will be 400 allowing for the above stipulated exigencies). Some of these will join our teacher training colleges, agricultural colleges and technical and commercial schools. Of course, we have got private Secondary Schools which now number over 300. And we feel that it is our obligation to supply them with enough graduate teachers.

Kyambogo at the moment produces 110 diploma holders every year. In five years' time, if it keeps up this rate, there will be 550 diploma holders plus the present 900 already in the field. This puts the number at roughly 1450. Research has shown that headmasters hesitate to take on Kyambogo graduates because they feel that they cannot easily call upon them to shoulder teaching responsibility in the whole secondary section. So, once there is a large enough supply of graduate teachers, unless they are forced by the Government, head teachers are hardly likely to engage these diploma holders and there will be frustration on the part of the latter. The owners of private schools, realising that these people have no alternative but to teach in their schools, may offer them low salaries - though now if they manage to persuade a few to join them, they pay them better salaries than the Government pays. Since we feel that it is the obligation of the Faculty of Education at Makerere to supply graduate teachers to the private secondary schools, it is not fair to think that after Kyambogo diploma holders have been rejected in Government Secondary Schools, they will be the ones to be pushed by necessity to these private Secondary Schools. So all wise suggestions should point in the direction of either stopping the diploma course at the Teachers National College, Kyambogo, which aims at supplying teachers for the Primary School if in future are required to be trained in such a way that they do have a diploma in education. Of course, the entry qualifications would need to be raised to Higher School Certificate level. This would work very well towards the raising of standards in the Primary Schools. Then, the final stage of accomplishment in the training of our teachers still awaited would be to require every teacher to have a degree before being allowed to teach in any of our schools. This aspiration may appear unattainable but it is bound to be discussed.

Graduate expatriate teachers and their contribution

In a further bid to cope with the shortage of graduate teachers for our Secondary Schools which became acute as a result of the unprecedented expansion of secondary education - the number of schools rose from 22 to 75 in the period 1960 - 1970 — the Uganda Government, like the Governments of Kenya and Tanzania, made an arrangement in 1960 with the British and the U.S.A. Governments to send here each year a considerable number of young graduates, straight from their home Universities, to be trained at Makerere for nine months and take up teaching positions in secondary schools after that. Their course of training led to the Diploma in Education (E.A). It was also arranged to have graduates from other parts of the Commonwealth, hence Australians participated in the programme, which was known as T.E.A. or Teachers for East Africa.

In 1969, Tanzania stopped taking T.E.A. teachers. However, the programme still continues for Uganda and Kenya and draws students from Britain and Australia but in diminishing numbers. American graduates have come under what is called the Peace Corps Scheme since 1965. Peace Corps teachers undergo a short orientation course of about six weeks and after that are posted to schools where they teach for periods ranging from a year to two years and then return to the U.S.A.

In the same year that the T.E.A. programme was instituted, the American and the British Governments launched another programme known as Afro-Anglo-American programme (A.A.A.), financed by the Carnegie Corporation, an American donor body, for the purpose of enabling qualified and experienced American and British teachers to come and participate in the task of training teachers south of the Sahara and north of the Limpopo. The programme, which is still in force, is administered at Teachers College, Columbia University, New York and has been responsible for the administration of a scholarship scheme whereby outstanding African graduates are enabled to pursue courses leading to higher degrees in the field of education, after which they return to their respective countries for teacher education work or for educational administration.

In 1969, A.A.A. changed its name to the Association for Teacher Education in Africa (A.T.E.A.) and in addition to its original role now gets leading teacher educators to meet once a year and discuss how they should run meaningful teacher education programmes and share ideas and experiences. The A.T.E.A. is now presided over by an African and at the time of writing it is intended that the chairman shall be an African educator. Teachers College, Columbia University, still plays a big part in the progress and activities of this association.

The Canadians and the Scandinavian countries, like Sweden and Norway, have assisted in providing teachers for secondary schools and teachers colleges. It should also be mentioned here that some headmasters and headmistresses have been free to recruit teachers for their schools, particularly from Britain.

It would be unreasonable not to appreciate the contribution made by expatriate teachers to the task of keeping our schools and colleges running and in coming to the rescue at the time of immense teacher shortage which, at one time, threatened our educational progress and made the country's man-power requirements unattainable, except in the distant future. However, it may be pointed out that in some places where the majority of the teachers are expatriates one sometimes cannot help suspecting that they still think that it is they who make things 'tick'. In some places and on some occasions, pupils tend to think that it is the expatriate teacher who teaches well and can run the school effectively. Of course, if this is true, it is a considerable challenge to the Uganda teacher to demonstrate in no uncertain terms his capability in the classroom and, indeed, in any field where he is called upon to shoulder responsibility.

It is well to mention that dependence on external sources for staffing secondary schools, in particular, has been attended by several problems which, on a number of occasions, have made the operation of schools far from easy. First of all, the short nature of the expatriate's tour of 21-24 months in many cases has not coincided with the end of the school's academic year so that it has not been uncommon to find that just in the middle of any given term a teacher has or teachers have to go on leave, sometimes to come back after 90 days or not to come back at all. As a result, classes have gone untaught for sometime. For science in particular, replacement has taken up to 6 months. Pupils without teachers and in a system where considerable importance is attached to performance in examinations reasonably become restive and pose intractable problems for school administration. Obviously, the short stay of expatriate teachers makes it more important for the Ministry of Education to draw up syllabuses and a clear policy and see to it that they are implemented.

Secondly, development of a curriculum with a strong local bias has been very slow to get under way and the tendency has been to rely as much as possible on the kind of curriculum with which the teacher recruited from overseas is familiar. Consequently, there is often criticism that what is taught is irrelevant to the Ugandan situation. Our hope is that when the Curriculum Development Centre gets off the ground and schools are staffed by Ugandan teachers there will be no more grounds for such criticism.

The Institute of Education

To better the courses for teacher education and to help to construct a progressive curriculum for all schools in the country and also to try out teaching materials and text books for schools, an Institute of Education was set up in 1949. But, unfortunately, for many years its role was not fully developed. Perhaps, it was unfortunate that when it was set up, it was headed by the Professor of Education who, although industrious, had too much work; it was his assignment to raise teacher training standards at the Faculty of Education which then and until recently was the only training centre for secondary teachers for the whole of East Africa. Organisation and administration of the Faculty apart with a small staff, he had to supervise areas in Uganda, Kenya and Tanzania, and to this add participation in activities which were then designed to develop Makerere into a University College for East Africa and, eventually into a University for Uganda. He was Professor of Education, Dean of the Faculty of Education, Head of the Department of Education and Director of the Institute of Education.

The Institute of Education was supposed to work on the improvement of the curriculum and syllabuses and assess suitability of text books and teaching materials. But it never, as far as we can find, concerned itself until recently with what was going on in primary teacher training colleges and primary schools, leaving this work to be carried out by the Inspectorate and missionary organisations (while they still controlled the schools). For secondary schools, syllabuses, text books and curriculum were decided by the Cambridge Overseas Examinations Syndicate. The Inspectorate dealt with Cambridge directly and made no reference to the Institute of Education.

To date, with the background sketched here, with the exception of few people, even at Makerere, to many people in this country it is not clear what the Faculty of Education is and what the National Institute of Education is, and what their respective roles are. The siting of both organisations does not help one to see the different roles at all since they are in the same spot, share a library, teaching rooms and offices and both train teachers.

Castle's Education Report strongly recommended that the Institute be concerned with the development of educational research, school curricula, syllabuses, and teacher education courses for the entire education system. However, even under a new dynamic and resourceful Director, the Government somewhat contrary to what the Castle Report had recommended curtailed the functions of the Institute. It was assigned to deal with the curriculum and syllabuses of primary teacher training colleges and to undertake the upgrading of a few grade 3 teachers to grade 4 and a few grade 4 to grade 5 and refresher courses, jointly with the Inspectorate for primary teachers. What should be the role of the Institute of Education in the 1970's? The authors think that the Institute would do well to undertake research into the education needs of this country, in the fields of primary, secondary, teacher, technical, adult, and even university education. The research into education needs of a developing country such as ours should be a detailed continuous process which can be carried out effectively and economically only by one organisation and this we think should be the Institute. It is also the feeling of the authors that the projected Curriculum Centre should be associated with the Institute very closely. Given time, the Institute ought to be a resource centre for aspects of education here. It should play a leading role in the educational system in Uganda.

4

The teacher in Uganda, past and present

Teachers emerge as leaders
When the professional teacher appeared on the scene in Uganda - teaching the catechism together with some writing and reading or teaching only the secular subjects - he was a man apart. It meant that he had mastered some of the knowledge brought by the white man and, unlike others who had also tasted that knowledge, he could even explain it to others in an intelligible and coherent manner. He was regarded as a different person from those others who had attended the lessons of the white man together with him.

Secondly, this teacher was the missionary's right hand man. The missionary realised that to spread Christianity rapidly he had to be in constant touch with this man, giving him guidance perhaps after work late in the evening, and sometimes visiting people with him. So, people, more and more, came to connect him with the white man, calling him his partner because he spoke about the new knowledge with relatively similar authority and enthusiasm. Part of the respect accorded to the white man went to the teacher.

The job involved a lot of persuasion of people so that they could see the benefit that was derived from sending their children to school. Consequently, the teacher had to have a persuasive approach and convincing attitude, accompanied by extreme kindness, in order to inspire trust and confidence in the people. All this behaviour was part of the training of the teacher and it was a miniature of what the missionary was also practicing. Thus, while the missionary's large home was teeming with enthusiastic people, old and young, who normally put up in it, that of the catechist and of the teacher was teeming with youngsters who lodged there and had their lessons during the day at the foot of the teacher, and improved their Christian behaviour according to the Christian deportment of the teacher and what he told them about God. These youngsters helped the teacher by cultivating his gardens and helped themselves by producing the food that fed them during the term, just as this was done in the Mission post of the missionary. The teacher did not feel that accommodation of such pupils in his home - some of whom where children of his relatives, others of his friends, and others of people with whom he shared none of these relationships - inconvenienced him at all. This was part of his job, just like the missionary who gathered a lot more of these people in his home; the relationship which he had with them was animated by the desire to win them to his master Christ and bring them up well schooled in Christian feeling as well as in the wisdom of this world, to help them change their way of living. In this way, the teacher was looked on also as a father by these children and a partner in the responsibility of bringing up their children by the people.

Besides, those young men and women who graduated from school continued to look at the teacher as a sort of parent, while at the same time, they continued to draw inspiration from him by seeking advice from him on certain matters connected with the African way of thought and how it could be absorbed in such a way that it did not conflict with the new Christian way of thought.

As the teacher walked through the villages also meeting those people who had not gone to school, he talked with them in an educative manner, trying to show them how they could improve themselves, thus putting them into a mood that would make them send their children to school eventually to gain the new knowledge. At social gatherings and anywhere there was some discussion and he happened to be around, he was always outspoken and people would expect him to say something. He would speak with confidence and because he had learnt how to meet people in discussion with no shyness, he would acquit himself well. He would meet the outspoken chief on equal ground who also respected him for he was the educator of his children, giving them the special knowledge that many people were now seeking in order to march with the times.

This trust and respect which the teacher won from the people at large, together with his outspokenness, was accompanied by a kind of affluence. This affluence was meagre indeed, especially if looked at in today's terms but it was bound to increase as time went on. As an example of how meagre it was, a teacher who was unqualified but who taught one of the authors well in a subgrade school back in 1935 was getting 5 E.A. Shs. a month; the certified teacher whom he joined in 1937 at a mission primary school fifteen miles away from home, in primary three, was getting 18 E.A. Shs a month. And, during all this time, the catechist teachers were being given about three kanzus a year to look tolerably decent and each of them got his yearly poll tax paid by the missionaries. Indeed, back in the early years of the establishment of our educational system, for example between 1898 and 1920, the monthly financial remuneration must have been very much smaller. But the point about it was that it was constant every month while the majority of the people did not have a constant income of any kind. Also, the teacher engaged pupils on his gardens and the produce from this, which was usually ample because many hands helped, was sold and brought in a good income. So, teachers easily paid their yearly poll tax, dressed perhaps smartly throughout the whole week, and besides the chiefs, they were the majority among those people who owned moderately modern houses.

When knowledge is accompanied by personal moderation, outspokenness and some kind of affluence above the majority of people around you, it excites confidence and trust in you and usually it turns you inevitably into a community leader. So, this is the way the teacher won a place of leadership in our society in the early period. It was not political leadership, however, though gradually from among them many were promoted to posts of political leadership in the Local Government administrations. But, by and large, they tended to be undisputed leaders of public thought and, with missionary backing, no one would fail to treat them as such.

At this early stage in the development of our educational system and of the new political administration and economic system, the teaching profession was the only honourable opening that offered unlimited opportunities for the majority of ambitious young men and women who attended school and who wanted to be employed afterwards. The political administration, headed by the Colonial Government, wanted only a few African clerks, interpreters, askaris and office messengers; so did the very few commercial establishments that were opening up. Chiefs tended to be sons of chiefs in most instances so that political posts in local administrations were generally left to rotate within a small circle of families. Thus, the teaching profession was the only large opening for the majority of the ambitious young men and women completing primary two, four or six. This was fortunate in that it also attracted the most brilliant men and women who could keep the standard of the profession fairly high. And, because it was very much coveted and it offered perhaps the best alternative of employment in the country, the employers could insist on high standard of entry and working; anybody failing to meet these two requirements would not be tolerated in the profession.

The gradual independence of the teacher
Before 1925, when the Government started to take a hand in the direction of the educational policies of the country, the teachers had no certificates granted by teacher training institutions as already mentioned. They taught because the missionaries had singled them out as outstanding pupils and joined to this was their desire and intention to teach. So, the absence of this certification tended to make these teachers more prone to doing whatever the missionaries demanded of them lest they should fall out of grace with the authorities who could suspend them from their jobs. Since the missionaries were the sole owners of schools with the exception of the army school at Bombo and Makerere Technical College set up in 1921, the African teacher had nowhere to transfer his service to from the missionaries' schools. Since it was only the good word of a missionary in one particular school that stood surety for a teacher (so that if he changed to another school without that person's recommendation, the other missionary could not take him on), the teacher was really subordinated and quite bound to do what his master, the missionary, told him to do, lest he lost that treasured employment. And, in particular, the teacher was stringently required by the missionary to be an outstanding example in his behaviour and by teaching. He had to attend church services without fail on Sundays and on holy days and to participate in

Christian discussions at the Mission. He would be expected to preside over prayers and songs in church for he was supposed to know more than the rest of the faithful. In social life he would not be expected to overstep the accepted Christian principals such as keeping one wife.

The certification of teachers from 1925, by the Government requiring them to attend teacher training schools, introduced a new element into the situation. This was the gradual independence of the teacher from subordination to the missionaries, because he felt that he could use his certificate to go and teach in another school if he fell out of favour with the missionary who was in charge of one school. But the situation was still complicated by the fact that the schools were broadly owned by two groups of Christian hierarchies: the Roman Catholic and the Church Missionary Society. A teacher brought up in the teachers colleges of one group and, who by religion also belonged to that denomination, would not be easily accepted to teach in the schools of the other group. So the certified teacher had still to continue being under considerable subordination to the missionaries, for the schools of each of the above hierarchies were controlled centrally and the centre had to be convinced that a particular teacher wanted to go from one school to another. But sometimes the centre would accept the transfer, and here it could rely more on the validity of the certificate which spoke for itself instead of, as previously, relying on the particular missionary, out of whose favour a teacher had fallen, to give a recommendation to such a teacher.

The Government also tended to feel that there was too much pressure brought to bear on teachers by the missionaries and, at the same time, it wanted to break through the strong wall of the missionaries' power in the running of schools. So, implicitly, it wanted to demonstrate to the teachers that it was on their side on occasions when there were complaints against the missionaries. It gave the impression that if a teacher had a certificate and that he was a competent and a reasonable person like any other citizen, the demand on him to act as a religious person should be relaxed, and that his social activities in his home were his own concern. Yet the missionaries would not accept this point of view entirely. The teacher should be a partner in the spreading of the word of God and in exemplary Christian behaviour so that his words in the school should match his behaviour out of it.

The more revolutionary teachers also put up a fight to see that there was a separation between their life at school and their life in public at the end of the teaching day. Moreover, they saw that the missionary paternalistic behaviour was not altogether for the benefit of the teacher, it worked to pressure him. For example, the missionaries had taken the view that teachers should not be paid their salaries during the three holidays a year when the pupils would be on holidays at home. Because this saved the Government money, the Government tended to agree with the missionaries. The teachers had to put up a struggle to see that they got paid by insisting that the holidays were forced on them by the missionaries and, if they wanted them to stay at school during holidays, they were prepared to do so. Yet, their European and American counterparts did not forfeit their salaries during the holidays. The point here which we want to stress is that certification encouraged the teachers to feel that they were now professional men and women who should be treated with due consideration befitting professional people and that once they had got a certificate, they should not be required to do duties that went beyond the job which they were supposed to do. Certification gave them courage to speak out and to start bargaining with their employers.

The rise of private schools and their effect on teachers

While this spirit of independence was developing among teachers, another kind of school was also developing: That was the independent private school. This type of school was pioneered by Ssebbanja Mukasa, now familiarly known as Father Spartas of Namuoona, and by Ernest Balintuma Kalibbala, now Doctor Kalibbala. Both of them quite controversial men, each in his own right, and the sort of men who could not accept the subordination and paternalism of both the missionaries and of the colonial administrators. These men were joined later on by Anselm Musoke, a trained teacher from Makerere, a short, little man but very dynamic and independent in thought. The schools, the first of which was opened in 1925 by Ssebbanja Mukasa, increased in number gradually from the 1940s. The owners, who were at their early time mainly rebellious teachers from the mission schools, wanted other teachers desperately; they started to woo those who had begun to feel that they could not continue in the missionary employment. Indeed, they were branded by the missionaries on leaving them as men who had failed in moral behaviour and professional proficiency and who were likely to do little good anywhere they went-to teach.

Besides this, the Muslim authorities had begun again by the 1940s to open up many primary schools for Muslim children, but they also lacked qualified primary teachers for reasons discussed elsewhere. The Muslim authorities readily took on Christian teachers who deserted Christian schools. Here the rigid demands of the missionaries did not apply to them. They taught secular knowledge and left the teaching of the Koran to the Muslim teachers. They acquitted themselves as good and reasonable citizens and were acceptable in the Muslim schools.

This spirit of assertion of their rights and desire to separate the job from personal life came to a head in early1940s. Teachers began to think in terms of a union or association that would be strong enough to bargain with both Government and the missionaries for terms of service and salaries as we shall see later. So, the 1940s marked a definite change from the period when a teacher was an apprentice of the missionary to a certified teacher and then, finally, asserted himself gradually as a person who should not be treated paternalistically.

The decline of the teacher's community leadership

While the above developments were going on, a different element was emerging in society which worked adversely on the community leadership which the teacher had won during the early period of the development of the educational system. By 1940, there were a large number of mission bred people in our society, brought up by the teachers in mission schools. Some of these people were in permanent employment. This had increased because the colonial administration and the local native administrations, plus the commercial sector, had grown much larger. Other mission bred people were cultivators or were employed in self employment of one kind or another. The remarkable characteristic about all these people was that they could easily express themselves in terms of the knowledge they had gained from schools, just like the teachers, the majority of whom had primary four education. The mission bred people were just as ready to speak out as the teachers and their affluence was the equal of the teachers in many respects and on the verge of outstepping it. Employment in the political administration and in the commercial sector tended to pay higher salaries to the employees while self-employed businessmen and hard working cultivators were also getting good financial remuneration from their activities. The salary of the teacher, although it had gone up a little from the days of the twenties and thirties, was still very low and relatively static. For example, the salary of the teachers trained after their primary four and that of teachers trained at Makerere College: ranged between 40 E.A. Shs and 90 E.A. Shs a month by 1945. So, it was no longer the teacher who paid his yearly poll tax promptly, who had a moderately fashionable home and who dressed better than the rest of the people among whom he moved. There were now many others like him who were not in his profession and he was no longer a person easily singled out where so many other people were now involved. When he talked with other people, it was on equal grounds for the knowledge which he was expressing and drawing upon to enter situations was the knowledge which also these other people had imbibed in schools to a large degree.

Secondly, the Second World War was also an eye opener. Thousands and thousands of semi-literate and literate men of the Protectorate from the age of eighteen up to 40 joined the Seventh Battalion of East and Central Africa (hence, the term in Luganda 'abaseveni', meaning men of the seventh battalion later on to be more familiarly known as the "Bakaawonawo" or veterans of the Second World War). These men all came back after the war with their horizons widened, knowledgeable and exceptionally outspoken. From the savings which they had made out of their gratuities, they were affluent in the society of that time (some of them had savings amounting to about two hundred shillings). The majority of them spent this money lavishly and impressed many people who had not gone to the war. The more shrewd among them invested it in one-man businesses and began running flourishing small concerns. These ex-service men recounted the experiences far and wide in the villages, like heroes, telling fantastic stories in which they were sharing the same habitation, food, cigarettes and death with the white man. They would tell people that they had seen some ignorant white men who were even sometimes under the command of Africans. This was unheard of or even dreamt of in a society that looked at any white man as a genius. These ex-service men added to a large group of men who came to frequent the same informed circles of men and, inevitably, became community leaders of public opinion.

Moreover, the staunch Christian way of looking at things was also losing its grip. It was no longer necessary for the teacher to go round villages persuading parents to send children to him. The majority anyway had realised that if their children had to cope with the new situation and be in a position to struggle for similar opportunities on equal terms with those who were attending schools, they had to send them to school, too. So, the teacher was confined to the school, coping with the numerous children who were coming to him; he was a rarity in the villages trying to influence public opinion and airing his knowledge. Though he continued to board a few pupils of relatives and friends, he kept the number very small and the majority of teachers stopped this practice for economic reasons. So, he narrowed his sphere of influence; many parents, once they had paid the school fees, would rather have nothing to do with the teacher.

Catechists continued their practice of visiting the faithful but they were no longer effective themselves in influencing public opinion because they continued to be recruited from those people who hardly knew how to read and write and they were quite a humble lot. As they continued to get no salary from the missionaries but clothing and money to pay their yearly poll tax, they were at quite a disadvantage both in academic refinement and personal possession of material goods. So, to many people their visits were more tolerated than welcome, and as on many occasions they turned up at a person's home to ask for church tithes (ndobolo) and contributions to help build the church or a school in an area over which the mission had jurisdiction or to try to advise Christians who had relaxed their Christian principles, their visits were often not welcome.

In a situation of the above nature, the kindness, the out-spokeness and relative affluence which had thrust natural community leadership onto the teachers disappeared into the background. But, during the governorship of Sir Andrew Cohen (1952-1957) who initiated elections to local Government Councils in order to get people used to electing their leaders, the teachers were found to be better prepared to organise their thoughts and to give more coherent speeches that made them dominate these Councils at the beginning. Otherwise, the teacher was no longer a more special person in his society than others. These other people, besides having attended school, had materially improved their social position to a greater extent than he had, especially by the 1950s.

The education of the primary teachers, who formed the majority of teachers in Uganda, was disastrous. When people had caught up with him by the 1940s, the teacher continued to be recruited at primary six up to the mid 1950s. Together with his low education went his low salary and poor accommodation. Those teachers with junior three qualifications who were teaching in primary five and six were also badly off in terms of salary and conditions of service, compared with their colleagues who had joined the Government service or who had gone to work in the commercial concerns. Those teachers with school cetificate qualification and who were teaching in the junior secondary section fared better in terms of salary and conditions of service if they were to be considered in terms of their classmates who either went straight on to work in Government departments or in the business world.

Although parents were eager to send their children to the teacher, for that was how they could get their fruits of education, they were not too keen on seeing them become teachers on their qualification at any stage of the educational system. Nor were many ambitious young men and women so inspired to join teaching by these salaries and poor conditions of service.

This was not all. Realising that the teaching profession was no longer an attraction for the students, the people in charge of running the educational system of the country lowered the standards of entry into the teacher training colleges. So, they took anybody who had gained a third class pass in the primary, the junior and in the senior secondary examinations. At the last two levels, even those who had not got certificates but had attempted the examinations, would be taken into training. The result was that students who were really wanted to enter the teaching profession whatever the grades they would have scored in those examinations, (those students who had scored the lowest grades and perhaps had very little liking for teaching, and those who had failed their examinations), were all bundled together and ushered into the teaching profession because the last two categories of people could not be accepted where they had originally wanted to go. These students indeed came to teaching feeling that it was a wrong profession for them but they had nothing to do. It was little related to their ambitions, interests and ability. No one but an idealist could think that such people were likely to rescue the teaching profession from its downward trend. In the face of this confusion of mind among those people who were at the forefront of directing our educational system, the teacher could not but lose his community leadership in influencing public opinion, if not even lose respect in the public eye. Those people with whom he had been studying would not fail to say, having got where they had got, that the teacher was remaining where he was because he had been tried and found unable to climb as far as them.

In the struggle to better their financial position and be less financially embarrassed, some of the teachers, indeed very few (and this needs to be stressed), began towards the end of the 1940s to run sundry businesses in the evening after work. They would either run a small shop or engage in driving their old cars as taxis or go into farming on a business scale. We feel strongly that the teacher had, and even now has, a right to use his free time in a way he sees to be most beneficial for his worldly prospects. But society had not expected this kind of thing from him; when the teachers' employers attacked it as unprofessional and said it was bound to lead to teachers being inefficient in their jobs, the public also looked at the teacher as a person who was neglecting his job of educating their children. A few of these commercially minded teachers could sometimes even snatch time to work in their taxi cab and carry people if they were between two close towns; or they could sneak out of school and do shopping to replenish their small shops. But these were very few. The majority of those teachers who engaged in one-man business activities carried out these activities after work and on non-teaching days. Both his employers and the public claimed that if the teacher could engage himself so, when could he mark pupils' exercise books and also prepare the following day's lessons? This kind of question arose from these people's experience of the teacher to whom they had been used during the thirties and early forties when perhaps he felt that his salary could satisfy his needs.

Yet, questions like these ones would have revealed to both society and the Government that a teacher's job was a unique one; it required him to devote his time to it most of the day and part of the night and, therefore, it would have been more in keeping to double or treble its financial remuneration and also to better his conditions of service. The teacher knew that a person working in an office was required to open his files at 8 a.m. and close them as soon as the clock struck 4 p.m. Yet the teacher would start working much earlier and go on into the night. From the human point of view, the teacher could either go on doing this - and grumbling - or he could also try to rationalise the situation and try to put in as much work as his fellow man working in an office put in. One could find a few teachers with this kind of mind who ran their sundry businesses but the majority laboured untiringly in the above manner.

To stop these few teachers from running such businesses, the Department of Education, and now the Ministry of Education, tried then (and also try today) to transfer such teachers. For example, if a man has got a shop in a certain locality, he is transferred to a place miles away where he cannot get into the shop in the evening. But normally this does not improve his morale so as to increase the energy he puts into the new school. He gets more distracted and disturbed. For he leaves his wife behind either to see to the running of the shop or the shamba or both and he goes home every Friday evening returning to the school late in the evening on Sunday. Yet many cases of such teachers which we have investigated show that they leave the school at midday on Friday and return to it at midday the following Monday because of transport problems. And if they find problems at home they may not be able to return before the middle of the next week.

Besides the fact of a few of his colleagues engaging in businesses, the teacher, towards the end of the 1940s, began to regard himself much like any other responsible citizen and took part in social activities of the community. But here society which had hitherto looked at him in connection with missionary activities, sometimes comparing him to a missionary who disavowed close connection with women, was shocked and all the special mysticism that still surrounded the teacher disappeared. Unfortunately, society usually exaggerated what the few teachers might have done to excess and took this to be the general behaviour of many teachers. So, a few teachers who might have gone to school drunk, or who might have misused school funds, or who might have misbehaved with school girls, tended to make parents lose confidence in teachers as a whole. Indeed, there is nothing so bad as generalising without careful research and then reaching water-tight conclusions. But this is not usually the concern of the general public. The mysticism that surrounded the teacher having completely disappeared, what remained then for him was to labour at his job like any other person - usually justifiably-disgruntled with his low salary and very poor conditions of service and, with no hope of ever getting his position bettered in the eyes of a society, which had now begun to associate special respectability with a person only if he grew richer every year. This fact could only be demonstrated by discarding the old bicycle for a motor cycle and, eventually, a motor car and then a more modern house.

The teachers' struggle to better their position

By the early 1940s, the teachers themselves had realised that society had caught up with them, and that it was fast leaving them behind unless they pulled themselves together to improve their position. This could be done in two ways: By their employers raising their salaries and bettering their conditions of service, and by they themselves keeping up to date so as not to lose their community leadership. But in both ways they had great obstacles to surmount. As regards bettering themselves academically this was largely out of their power because if those people responsible for recruiting teachers continued to recruit them mainly at primary level and even engaged unqualified teachers, the teachers would still be at a low academic level. Indeed, they could insist on getting up-grading and refresher courses but these had their limitations. After all, if a person had only Primary School education those who had left him behind and joined Secondary Schools would still treat him as a man of primary education despite his having undergone the above course later on. Though, of course, those teachers who taught primary five and six and junior secondary education and those from Makerere, who had full secondary education and above, tended to be fewer than those teachers teaching below primary five. So, they were swamped by the number who were even more to be seen in villages than in town. Moreover, their salaries did not help to raise them above these large numbers.

As far as raising teachers' salaries, the Government and the missionary bodies were not keen to listen to this plea. First of all, the teaching profession had always employed the largest number of people in this country. So, the Government and the missionaries were frightened at the idea of raising the salaries of so many people. Secondly, even if they were brought around to agreeing to a rise, such a rise would be negligible in terms of a single teacher though it would run to a very large sum collectively. For example, in 1953 the salary of 30,000 Primary School teachers and Junior Secondary teachers was raised. The highest rise was 20 E.A. Shs and the lowest was 5 E.A. Shs for a person per month. Such rises really made little difference to an individual's financial position, but the Government had to add 300,000 E.A. Shs a month to the teachers' salary bill as a whole.

In the early forties, however, whether any rise in the salary would really affect an individual teacher little or much was not the question. The question was that teachers needed higher salaries than they were getting; so their employers were asked to make a move in this direction. This was accentuated by the rise in the cost of living occasioned by the war. So, their static and low salaries could no longer enable them to meet their financial obligations. Moreover, due to this rise in the cost of living nearly all workers both in Government and private bodies began to get salary increases in the early forties. Because they were treated as civil servants, European and American teachers got salary increases, too.

The teachers realised that they needed to combine with the missionaries for better salaries and better conditions of service; in this way they hoped to be listened to. But to unite was not all that easy. There were tribal animosities and denominational differences which presented problems. Yet, there were some teachers who realised that such small niceties could be overcome easily by tactful leadership because the grievances of the teachers were too great to ignore. At a first attempt to bring teachers together into one organisation, a group of teachers working at Nabumali High School near Mbale formed in 1942 a small organisation which they called the African School Teacher Association (A.S.T.A.). Unfortunately, the first teachers to organise this body and those who joined it subsequently were all Protestants and other teachers in that area from the Roman Catholic group were reluctant to join it. However, this did not deter the association from functioning. It still hoped that the differences which prevented the Catholics from joining them would disappear if benefits could be gained as a result of these teachers having come together.

The example of the teachers in Mbale was followed by those around Kampala in 1944. These teachers, because they were in a metropolitan area, had a great deal of support from those who had little interest in such niceties as tribal and denominational differences. So their organisation to which they gave the name of the Uganda African Teachers Association (U.A.T.A.) had from the beginning a large following. They contended that if you were an African teacher you were a teacher whatever the area of Uganda from which you accidentally happened to come and the religion through which you worshiped your God. The question of the day was how to better teacher's salaries, conditions of service, and the self re-education of teachers.

At once the Uganda African Teachers Association sat down to make a constitution, which focused its attention on the real glaring problems that faced the African teachers in Uganda, and suggested the best ways of removing them. That constitution was published in 1945 and had the following main items in it:

To unite all teachers in Uganda.

To promote and maintain the interests of the teaching profession and to safeguard the interests and welfare of its members.

To render the teaching profession attractive to the rising generation of Uganda.

To secure the solidarity of teachers and extend the influence of the teaching profession.

To affiliate with local, national and international bodies connected with or interested in the education of the child.

To maintain a high standard of qualification, to raise the status of the teaching profession, and to ensure that all the posts in the educational services of the country are open to members.

To provide means for the co-operation of teachers and the expression of their collective opinion upon matters affecting the interests of education and the teaching profession.

To enable members to receive fair treatment in whatever part of Uganda they may be and under whatever institution they may be working.

To associate with or assist the promotion of mass literacy, adult education and the education of the handicapped.

To purchase, lease property, alter and maintain any building required for the association.

To hold debates, lectures, talks and election competitions with a view to promoting and advancing the educational, cultural and literacy faculties of the members.

To make representatives to the Government and local authorities to invoke their aid for safeguarding and promoting the moral, social and economic life of the members.

To watch the administration of Pension Regulations and to endeavour to secure their amendment where necessary.

To assist an undertaking or company providing or about to provide life assurance for the benefit of members.

To secure, promote and maintain Teachers' Benevolent and Orphan Fund.

Armed with such a forward looking constitution, the leaders of the Uganda African Teachers Association toured the country persuading other teachers to join them in an effort to bring pressure to bear on both the Government and the missionaries. As a result, they got many teachers to join regardless of their ethnic group and denominational affiliations.

Although the Government had accepted and welcomed the formation of U.A.T.A., the Missions, which actually controlled the schools, did everything they could to ensure that it did not become established with too many members in their schools. They were very suspicious of its motives. They felt that if teachers belonged to one body they would become too militant and, consequently, would be more difficult to control. But the more the Missions objected to U.A.T.A, the more the teachers came forward to register as members; they felt that there were many things which needed to be improved, regarding their salaries and conditions of service, and the above constitution had put their case clearly before them.

To counterpart the influence of U.A.T.A., the Missions started denominational teachers organisations whose members were forced to submit to the wishes of the churches under which they served. The Catholic Teachers Guild (C.T.G.) began in this way in the 1940s in the Rubaga Diocese and it has survived the longest under the name of 'Agali Awamu', implying the solidarity of Catholic teachers and church leaders, whose aim was to discover how best they could co-operate to improve Catholic education. The Guild still exists and it is said to promote the social welfare of its members. But it has never involved itself in bargaining with the employers about the rights and privileges of its members. During the vital days of the struggle for improvement of the teachers' conditions of service and their salaries, the Catholic hierarchy used its influence to see that teachers who supported their point of view led the different branches of the Guild in the various parts of Uganda. This only helped to drive the more militant teachers into the ranks of the Uganda African Teachers Association. Seeing that they could not prevent Catholic teachers from joining the Uganda Teachers Association, the Catholic hierarchy allowed Catholic teachers to join it in the end - though they were still required to continue their membership in the Catholic Teachers Guild.

Although the Uganda African Teachers Association claimed to be the teachers organisation for the whole of Uganda, in fact this was not the case until about 1953. Before then its members were mainly teachers from the Buganda area. The Uganda African School Teachers Association in Mbale continued to operate until 1953. Although it was independent from the Uganda African Teachers Association the two groups consulted each other on the action to be taken on common problems such as teachers' salaries and conditions of service. In 1953 the Uganda School Teachers Association dissolved, and its members joined the Uganda African Teachers Association since its leaders saw no benefit in operating two separate bodies which had the same objectives and interests. In 1958, the name was changed to Uganda Teachers Association (UTA) when it was realised that there were many teachers of other races, such as Asians teachers, who would benefit by becoming members. These had their own teachers' organisation but at independence time, they realised that such associations were likely to be ineffective, if not undesirable, especially as the Government declared openly that it recognised only one teachers organisation: the Uganda Teachers Association.

The development of the Uganda African Teachers Association and later on the Uganda Teachers Association was impeded in the early 1950's by a disagreement between some teachers teaching in primary and in what was known as Junior Secondary Schools, on one hand, and those teaching in the Senior Secondary and Teacher Training Schools on the other hand. The former group of teachers felt that the leadership of the association was concentrated too much in the hands of the latter group. And it was alleged, as a result of this, that their interests were not being adequately represented to the Government. In fact, Makerere-bred teachers and teachers educated abroad and who were teaching in both Teachers Colleges and in Senior Secondary School tended to occupy all the key posts in the Association. In addition to this, they had quite good salaries, good houses in boarding schools and other ancillary benefits which were not obtainable by the Primary and Junior Secondary teachers who were nevertheless in the majority. So the latter group of teachers got the impression that such well-off people were not likely to press hard enough for the needs to their lower paid colleagues - like raising their salaries, giving them loans for at least buying motor cycles, and obtaining better accommodation at school (which was appalling at this time).

The disagreement grew worse and the Primary and Junior Secondary Schools teachers pulled out of the association in 1956 and, subsequently, registered themselves as the Vernacular Primary and Junior Teachers Union (V.P.J.U). Both the Union's title and its constitution, which will not appear here, left no room for any other grade of teachers above the Junior Secondary teachers. In 1965, it changed its name to the Uganda Teachers Union to try to attract teachers above that grade and so look less sectional.

Whilst U.A.T.A. and the V.P.J.U. had very similar objectives (and later U.T.A.) have always tried to function as a professional organisation and less as a trade union, by placing emphasis equally on the teacher and on the child. But V.P.J.U. and, later on U.T.U, argued that it existed for its members only - after all if the members were happy, the children would also gain because the teachers' morale would be high and they would thus be able to care for the children better.

The Uganda Teachers Union had quite a big following for the first few years after it had broken away from the Uganda Teachers Association but its membership dropped throughout the 1960s. It considered merging with the Uganda Teachers Association in 1967 but agreement could not be reached between the two organisations. The Uganda Ministry of Education, however, has publicly shown that it does not recognise the Uganda Teachers Union because its approach to education is not professional. It behaves like a trade union which may even call on its member to stage strikes. Thus, the Uganda

Teachers Union find it difficult to operate without formal Government support and it has been gradually losing members. However, it still exists and makes its vague presence felt through very short and occasional press releases and circulars sent to schools, and this usually happens as a retaliation to any public discussion held by the secretariat of U.T.A.

Despite the split in 1953, however, the Uganda African Teachers Association and now the Uganda Teachers Association developed steadily gaining more and more members even from the splinter groups who now realised that the solution to their problems was to be more militant within the mother association. And, indeed, as a result the leadership began to be shared without bias towards a particular section of the educational system and depended on qualities of leadership alone.

In 1962, U.T.A re-organised itself to operate more effectively and to reach teachers more quickly in all the corners of Uganda. It set up a secretariat headed by a permanent secretary. As a result of this it has built up a strong machinery. Now two thirds of the Teachers in Uganda belong to it and, as a result of teachers coming together in one strong organisation, they have achieved many good things. The following are some of the achievements that have been gained since the teachers formed their organisation:

(i) Teachers' salaries have improved considerably since 1940 and a pensions scheme was set up after a long struggle.
(ii) Teachers, through their organisation, are represented on educational committees and the school boards such as the Teaching Service Commission and the Salaries Advisory Committee.
(iii) Teachers can go on refresher courses organised and run by their organisation.
(iv) Conditions of service have improved and are still improving.
(v) Teachers have one employer now after almost twenty years of hard fighting for it.
(vi) Teachers have learnt to save by buying insurance policies through their own scheme and by being encouraged to join credit unions.
(vii) Teachers in Uganda are consulted by the Government on educational matters through their own organisation.
(viii) Their organisation has put up a very impressive building in Kampala and has also built up a good library service in that building which helps teachers to improve their academic and professional abilities.

Indeed, as an individual, a teacher can do little compared with what can be achieved if he is a member of a teachers' organisation. Then he has every chance of making a valuable contribution to the cause of education in his country. Teachers' organisations are now the main instruments through which teachers can influence the educational planning and policy of every nation.

PART THREE

EDUCATIONAL ADMINISTRATION: PRACTICES AND TRENDS

5

The structure of the education system

Introduction
In this chapter, we describe in outline the structure of the system of education and mention and discuss briefly some of the problems in the system. In the chapters that follow, its administration will be described.

Generally, since 1925, the system of education has kept within the scope of what a British Government White Paper on Education in Tropical Africa described as a complete educational system. The White Paper in question said:

A complete educational system should include primary, including infant education, secondary education of different types, technical and vocational schools and institutions 'some of which may hereafter reach university rank' for such subjects as teacher education, medicine, agriculture and adult education.

It is true there have been further developments and modifications in the system in response to changing circumstances and the growing needs of Ugandans. But every year, problems such as that of unemployed primary school leavers assume such magnitude that we cannot help thinking that there is something wrong with the form of education system in this country.

The main formal divisions in the Uganda education system.

1. Primary
Here, as expected, emphasis is on the needs of childhood. Since 1965 the course lasts 7 years. While parents are not unwilling to let children go to school, the fact is that there aren't enough schools to absorb all Primary School age children and, even if we had the places, there would still not be teachers to man the schools.

Since independence, Primary School intakes in particular, have grown so rapidly year after year that there is now public agitation over the Primary School leavers without employment. But, note that these should be regarded as extremely privileged for having been through school while thousands of children of the same age remain at home.

The problem of Primary School leavers has brought the system of education under fire. Some suggestions in connection with this problem appear to make their authors sound indifferent and extremely impersonal. Primary School leavers should return to the land to start farming as it has been suggested. But whether the farming referred to is to be primitive or scientific is not specified; it is hard to imagine a 13-year old girl or boy opening up a shamba. Furthermore, although it is known very well that probably no more than, say, 15 per cent of Primary School children will get places in a Secondary School, the basis of Primary School education is the preparation for entry to Secondary Schools.

Circumstances at present are such that Primary Schools are frequently viewed as little more than sorting grounds whereby potential candidates for further education are sorted out and prepared for higher levels of education. The Primary School does not provide a suitable terminal education for the present job market in Uganda. It is very sad that the 85 per cent who do not go beyond Primary School are referred to by parents, and indeed by all of us, as those who failed to enter Secondary School. Our attitude, the public's attitude, makes it difficult for the majority of Primary School leavers to feel that they are of any worth in our society.

A crucial question is what can be done to bridge the gap between what the Primary School teaches and what the economy requires and, therefore, what the employer requires. This question has assumed great seriousness as the limitations which beset primary education as it is now in Uganda become apparent. It is disconcerting to think that the country may sooner or later have to face the disruptive potential of large reservoirs of disgruntled Primary School leavers. Finding means to channel their energies positively and check rising dissatisfaction calls for priority attention.

Two further questions are being asked: First, is the Primary course as it stands in the system a suitable introduction to a working life in Uganda? And second, what should be built into the structure of the system of education here to bridge the gap between leaving Primary School at the age of 12 or 13 and being ready for skilled training or employment at the age of 17 or 18.

A number of suggestions have been made. For instance, it has been suggested in some quarters that the education given in Primary School must be a complete education in itself, not just a preparation for entering a Secondary School. But can you achieve a complete education in seven years? We suppose that to do so you would have to make children work quickly, write quickly and calculate quickly. But, to seek speed in performance of school work when the whole mental and emotional machinery is undergoing a transformation and is correspondingly fragile, would certainly imply unacceptable disregard of the most elementary laws of biology and psychology. If you try to make a baby walk too soon you deform its legs. One of the roles of the Primary School is to teach children to work well and, for this purpose, it is essential to comply with the pace of performance that is suited to them. It seems that more than seven years would be needed to make primary education complete in itself. But then some authority would have to tell us in simple terms the ingredients that would make primary education complete in itself.

Regarding what should be built into the structure to bridge the gap between leaving the primary school at the age of 12 or 13 and being ready for training or employment or shortening the teenage gap as some people have called it, some two suggestions have been made: (a) Two years should be added to the course, making it of 9 years' duration, and (b) Delay entry to age 8.

The question is: Are these the answers to the problems? The first one, to begin with, does not seem to be practicable in terms of money and staffing. Furthermore, it raises a painful and tricky problem of giving nine years education to some children when a large number, thousands, cannot go to Primary School at all. But raising entry age to eight merits careful consideration - although we would need to find out about the educational effects of entry age before applying the proposal with confidence. To our knowledge and experience, some boys are 18 or 19 years old by the time they finish the course but, many times, they are in no better position than the 13-year old boys. Some of them do not even pass the Primary Leaving Examination nor do they appear rapidly employable.

But if it became necessary and practicable to add two years to the existing primary course as suggested, there is a strong case for supplementing the course with low cost agricultural or craft courses as this kind of training can be of immediate application in the area where the school is situated. There is strong feeling that the present Primary School programme should be replaced by a programme which is deliberately drawn up to bear direct relation to the agricultural economy and rural life of Uganda. Uganda is not and, in the foreseeable future, will not be a country of urban communities.

2. Secondary or Post Primary

All courses at this level last four years or six years in some cases. Programmes at this stage have to provide the pupil with general education that is, education aimed at the all-round development of the student, training him / her to think clearly and to develop desirable qualities of character. It is also at this stage that an attempt is made to give instruction that prepares a student for a job, if possible. It is very widely held among educators that vocational education should be supported by a good, firm general education. For this reason, one of the problems that have troubled authorities administering education in this country is how to have an effective vocational education and at the same time an effective general education. A number of experiments have been tried. For instance, in some schools vocational subjects have been added to general subjects. Yet other schools have been given programmes that have turned them into institutions with an agricultural or technical bias. However, it is possible to report that students have come out of these schools prepared for vocational employment. Indeed, some schools with technical or agricultural biases have been put back on to the usual Secondary School courses.

As indicated earlier in this book there has been rapid expansion of Secondary School enrolments since independence. First, as a result of the social demand for secondary education generated by its past economic benefits to its recipients, and secondly, as a result of the Government's need for high-level personnel. Secondary Schools are still growing, but year after year, it is becoming crystal clear that the market now is limited and the unemployed Secondary School leaver is a great headache to the Government and to parents.

Not long ago, the greatest number of Secondary school leavers found something to do when they left school. Some went into institutions of further education while others easily found employment. But of late, the emergence of a large surplus of S4 leavers that can neither go on to further education nor get employment is extremely worrying to us all.

The Secondary School section of our education system has been subjected to severe criticism. It has been suggested that there is a lack of direct relationship between the Secondary School and the area where it happens to be. What are the grounds for saying this? For instance, Secondary Schools are generally boarding schools, isolated as completely as possible from the surrounding community.

In most cases, schools have rules which restrict contact of their students with the community around, let alone the fact that many such schools are enclosed by wire fences with guarded iron gates. All visitors to the school sign a book before going through the gate stating the reason for the visit.

It has been further suggested that this particular section of the country's education system has continued to exist in a form that has not been adjusted to the changed circumstances in which the school leavers has to look for employment. The training the Secondary School gives prepares the student for further academic work but not for immediate employment when he / she leaves school. An employer who wants a typist wants a man who can type. He is not interested in a chap who cannot type, but can impressively quote from one or two of the set books. It has been suggest that in this country, the labour force seems to be growing by about 50,000 to 70,000 a year. The Secondary School leaver is in this force. The economy, on the other hand at the present rate (1971/72), can absorb only between 15,000 and 20,000 people a year. The thing is that to get the Secondary School leaver into this employable group, Secondary Schools must be re-organised, the curriculum diversified, and as announced in August 1971, the quality of teaching must be improved and linked more closely to human resources needs.

What can really be done? As usual, there has been no lack of answers to this question (there are always many self-appointed advisers on anything educational). We have been told that we should introduce, at our Secondary Schools, courses based on problems of development. Further, that we should conduct research to ascertain more about career destinations of Secondary School students of all types. Also, that we should run vocational guidance services at each Secondary School in order to be able to develop meaningful vocational programmes. To us this seems to be another list of theoretical propositions which carry no key to the problem which is with us right now. The question posed above still remains and has repercussions on educational administration.

Re-organisation and expansion are taking place in the area of technical and commercial education; this is very much welcome. For a long time, technical and commercial education, not only in this country but throughout East Africa, has been considered by many people as suitable for those who are not good enough for the usual type of school - the kind from which boys and girls matriculate into University, for instance. This attitude must be changed and our hope is that the re-organisation and expansion will be such that it will give us, in the shortest possible time trained workers for activities that stimulate the economy to generate more employment and more income. It should be made possible for a student to go to Makerere University through a technical or commercial institution.

There are also, in the educational system of Uganda, a number of institutions operating between S4 level and University. Some of these are:

(a) Higher School Certificate Institutions - providing two year courses in science or arts subjects.
(b) Agricultural Colleges which conduct a three year Diploma course in Agriculture
(c) Teacher Education Colleges of which National Teachers College at Kyambogo is a good example.

As far as students and parents are concerned, the first of the above mentioned institutions is the most popular of the lot. Doing the H.S.C. or E.A.A.C.E. course is the aim of the majority of S4 students, for it is the door to University. Here again, expansion of intake for H.S.C. since 1962 has been spectacular, to the extent that there is very little problem in filling places available at the University. However, there are three main problems associated with this section in our educational set up:

(i) Here we mean the great numbers at some schools who, after the two year course, fail to satisfy the examiners. Thus, time and money is wasted. To be fair, one should perhaps say that the failure of these students may be due to factors beyond their control, for example, ineffective teaching, lack of facilities, such as up-to-date laboratory equipment, inadequate pre-H.S.C. preparation, particularly in science. There are, of course, cases where the cause of failure is lack of application and disproportionate allocation of time to things that have nothing to do with the prescribed course.
(ii) The scope of choice of subjects is limited because resources do not permit a wider choice.
(iii) The time spent on the course is now inadequate; the results of the examination on which selections are based come late and the machinery for selection is slow. But an effort is being made to speed it up.

At the time of writing this account, institutions which for the last years or so have been producing teachers without degrees for teaching in Secondary Schools seem to be coming nearer and nearer to the end of their usefulness. At the rate Makerere is going to turn out graduate teachers, there will shortly be no justification, as we have already indicated, for employing non-graduates in Secondary Schools for the normal courses. It would be advisable for such institutions to specialise in areas like In-Service courses and preparation of teachers for the Primary Schools.

3. University.

Makerere University is the apex of the education system here. The story of its development over the years was told earlier in this book and, therefore, our remarks here will be confined to its role in the social and economic reconstruction of Uganda.

One of the biggest problems which faced and still faces independent Uganda was and still is the lack of high-level personnel which is required in the process of social and economic development. There is still need for an increased intake at our University - (1972) - for our human resources requirements still remain unfulfilled. But then, after saying that, one would be told of graduates who recently have not gained employment for a month or two after graduation in March. Some people have gone as far as suggesting that there may one day be a huge surplus of unemployed graduates. This suggestion cannot be disregarded nor is it correct to call it alarmist. We think it should stimulate us to ask a few questions about the University here.

First, should Makerere University go on performing the traditional functions which the Universities of Europe (on which it is patterned) have for many years performed for their people, viz. providing a liberal education? If so, for how long? Secondly, should Makerere University not now take on additional functions which, while radically distinguishing it from older European Universities, fit it nevertheless for greater and more relevant services to Uganda society? Thirdly, can Makerere effectively cope with the immediate and urgent demands on it for the improvement of our society and, at the same time remain loyal to world standards of Universities?

These questions may be answered in a number of ways by different people but, we think, there would be a considerable degree of agreement on a number of points regarding Makerere University. These points briefly are:

(i) Our University, like other universities elsewhere, has the responsibility to advance the frontiers of knowledge through teaching and research. Our University cannot afford to deviate from these traditional functions without degenerating into a second-rate institution, with consequent loss of international identity.

(ii) While providing a broad and liberal education, our University must of necessity lay stress on courses that will give us men and women with skills that will enable them to participate fully, immediately, and effectively in the economic and social development of the country.
(iii) It must endeavour to identify, define and confirm the aspirations of our society. It must research into Uganda's heritage.
(iv) It should endeavour, as far as is feasible, to adapt the content of its teaching and research specifically towards Ugandan and East African problems.

In summary, Makerere University must rise to the challenge of being the main instrument of national progress and the voice of Ugandans in the international councils of technology and scholarship. To rise to this challenge, the University must enjoy the fullest freedom to teach and research. In few words, it must enjoy full academic freedom.

Some stumbling blocks in Uganda's system of education

Observers of our education set up have pinpointed several disadvantages inherent in it. One of these is the existence of common examinations. The common examinations at primary and secondary level tend to standardise the education provided in Uganda. This we have been told may be good in some ways but bad in others - in that such examinations prescribe strictly what should be taught, and how it shall be taught and, therefore, could easily stifle teachers' initiative and the development of a spirit of enquiry on the part of pupils. Another disadvantage mentioned is this: Not much thought as yet has been given to the critical question, 'What kind of Ugandans should schools and University help to produce?' This question is obviously a difficult one but we cannot say that it is not receiving attention.

Corrections to imbalances in the education system

Recently, our leading educators and scholars of education have emphasised the role of what has been called non-formal education in meeting this need. Non-formal education has been defined briefly as 'skill and knowledge generation which takes place outside the formal school system'. Some of the men who repair cars in town have never been inside a classroom but they do the job and do it well. Outside the school system men are learning by actually doing - they accomplish tasks by association with others. It has been suggested that reasonable results could be obtained by causing non-formal education to take place through: (a) programmes of a practical nature aimed at improving employed human resources; (b) providing on-job training of craftsmen; (c) radio classes, homemaking classes; (d) weekend vocational workshops. This is a field worth exploring and it is our hope that the suggestion will be examined carefully and sincerely.

In these pages we have tried to sketch the education system as briefly as the compass of this book permits. In the coming pages, this will be followed by a description of the machinery that has been set up to administer it and will show how men and women responsible for its administration try to cope with the problems it poses.

6

Administration of education at Ministry and District levels

Introduction

Schools and indeed all educational institutions are service organisations. Sociologists define a service organisation as 'an organisation whose primary beneficiary is the part of the public in direct contact with the organisation. It is an organisation whose basic function is to serve its clients.'

In general, service organisations place emphasis on (a) providing professional services; (b) the welfare of the clients. In any service organisation, it is safe to assume that the client does not know what will best serve his interest. He is in the hands of the professional. He is not qualified to evaluate the services he needs. A pupil, for instance, cannot tell the school what knowledge he requires and in what doses. Professional educators have to determine what and how the pupils are to be taught, where, when and for how long.

This is obviously an administrative process, which, to use the language of administrators, includes decision-making, programming, communicating, controlling and reappraising.

Patterns of organisation, particularly of an educational system or an institution, must be such that they permit of a cycle of action, including the activities mentioned above. Patterns of organisation should be such that the system is easy to administer efficiently. In education administration, and here by administration we mean all that is done at the Ministry or District level or at school level to try to satisfy pupils' needs with due regard to the available resources; administrative efficiency is a matter of crucial importance.

In the literature on administration in general, efficiency receives lengthy discussion. The ideal is to maximise efficiency. But, if this be regarded as unattainable, some ways of enhancing administrative effectiveness are indicated. Three of these are:

(i) Arranging the members of the group in a definite hierarchy of authority to ensure unity of command and to eliminate confusion and irresponsibility.
(ii) Providing for specialization of the duty among the group in the direction that will lead to greater efficiency.
(iii) Keeping to the minimum the number of levels through which a matter must pass before it is acted on.

These three principles here briefly mentioned, it seems to us, have been consciously or unconsciously applied to the administration of education and, to the present organisation of the system at Ministry level in Uganda.

Present organisation of the system at Ministry level

First of all, a separate Ministry of Education has been in existence since independence. Without hesitation it can be stated that it is the largest of all the Ministries. It is also not an exaggeration to suggest the Minister's portfolio is not any easy one. Through his Ministry, the Government has to try as much as possible to satisfy the thirst of Ugandans for education and, for more and more education. As you know education is one of the services everybody claims to know something about. There is also no lack of self-appointed experts who would not hesitate to claim they have better answers to problems than the people actually involved in the service.

Let us now have a brief look at the structure of the Ministry and at the duties assigned to its main officials. There are six divisions now in the Uganda Ministry of Education.

1. Office of the Minister

Minister. This is a cabinet post. He is responsible for the administration of the Ministry, exercises direction and control and is responsible to the President. He has an assignment of considerable magnitude and complexity.

Permanent Secretary. He holds a civil service post, is charged with the organisation and operation of the whole Ministry, tenders advice in respect of the business of the Ministry, implements the policy of the Government, and is responsible for the proper expenditure of public money as allocated to the Ministry.

2. Financial and Establishment Division

Obviously this is a very important division, indeed. The Ministry handles a lot of money. For example, for the financial year 1970/71 E.A. Shs. 279,678,000 was allocated to the Ministry for current expenditure. To this, add E.A. Shs. 72,058,000 for capital expenditure in the same financial year. If you visit the Accounts section, you will see a lot of busy officers checking claim forms, verifying and examining all expenditure vouchers prior to payment, delving into correspondence concerning student loans, and preparing cheques for grants to schools and the University. Their work may be interesting but it is also really arduous.

As the Ministry employs many people, an Establishment Section has been set up with a Senior Establishment Officer to supervise and to organise the section, to handle personal and confidential matters affecting senior staff. A number of Higher Executive Officers deal with things like leave, passage, travelling allowances, housing for staff, appointments and terms of service, papers for expatriate staff, and local staff. Some officers are in charge of schedules that cover confidential registries, routine National questions, pensions, gratuities and workmen's compensation, plus educational subsidies.

3. Higher Education Division

We suppose every student knows about this. Officers in this division handle scholarship applications and payments of bursaries for University students. Even as a private student you have to go through their office if you want information over courses abroad or assistance in seeking placement at schools away from this country.

4. Schools and Colleges Division

This is probably the best known of all divisions of the Ministry. The duties of the Chief Education Officer whose office is in this section of the Ministry, clearly indicates the range, the scope and the variety of the operations of this division.

Chief Education Officer – C.E.O.

In most up-to-date literature on staff duties from the Ministry, he is described as Senior Professional Executive, advising the Minister and Permanent Secretary on all aspects of education, educational institutions and staffing. He co-ordinates and supervises schools and colleges. The Education Act 1970, by its provisions, makes clear the role and powers of the C.E.O. All education officers and inspectors of schools are under his direction. He may according to the Act, by notice published in the gazette, appoint any public officer to be an inspector of schools. He registers and licences persons who have completed a course of training approval by the Ministry responsible for education, if they apply. He is also empowered by the same Act to remove a teacher from the register if so advised for reasons listed under clause 13. According to the Act he now registers, classifies and closes private schools whose owners contravene the provisions of the Act.

For efficiency and promptness in handling problems that arise, there are a number of officers under the C.E.O. with clearly defined schedules. The one that most new teachers are likely to meet is the Senior Education Officer, Secondary Schools. He arranges for staffing of Secondary Schools, deals with recruitment of teachers, advises on aspects of Secondary Schools development and, in liaison with the Inspectorate, can take appropriate executive action on professional matters. In addition to S.E.O. Secondary Schools, there are headquarters Education Officers for primary education, teacher education, technical, farm and commercial education, careers guidance, and private schools. All these submit to the Chief Education Officer and operate as he directs executively and professionally.

5. Schools and Colleges Inspectorate Division

Headteachers, particularly, find school inspection very useful. Inspections are occasions for very valuable reappraisal of the teaching and the organisation of the school; a reappraisal which otherwise, amidst the daily hustle of school life, tends never to be made. The Inspectorate has an important role to play in assisting schools and in maintaining standards. The Ministry of Education has an Inspectorate Division with the Chief Inspector of Schools as its head.

One problem which this important division has had for some time is that it has been seriously understaffed. A staff list, not a long time ago, indicated really tightly packed schedules for Inspectors. For instance, Mr. X. the Senior Inspector of Schools had this type of schedule:

Head of Secondary Schools Section of the Inspectorate. Responsible for arranging the inspection of Secondary Schools and for advising the C.I.S. on all matters relating to Secondary education. Equating of certificates. Recommending confirmation of U.T.S. secondary teachers and award of final certificates. Adviser on matters connected with Secondary Schools building plans and furniture and equipment. Karamoja Development Plan, Inspection of evening classes. Responsible to C.I.S. for annual confidential reports on heads of Secondary Schools. Biology and Geography specialist; Inspector and adviser on matters relating to these subjects. Member of Examinations Committee, C.S.C. Panels for Biology and Geography. Member of Primary Leaving Examination Board. Matters concerned with agriculture in schools.

Since the beginning of 1969, a very big effort has been made to get an Inspector for each subject and there has been considerable success; this is glad news. The Inspectorate also covers the Schools Broadcasting Unit, a School Meals Unit, a Book Production Unit, and the Examinations Section. The amount of work the Examinations Section undertakes is increasing every year, because of the ever rising number of candidates. There is a lot of paper, sorting out mistakes made on entry forms by candidates, teachers and headmasters, preparing for the publication of results, answering questions from angry candidates and anxious parents - which all call for sacrifice on the part of the staff manning the section and on the part of the Chief Inspector of Schools who is responsible for examination and everything connected with them.

6. Planning and Statistical Division

The officer heading this unit is charged with responsibility for development planning, plan implementation, and maintaining liaison with the Ministry of Planning and Economic Development. He also prepares applications for financial assistance from external bodies. With the massive building programme, there has been for the last ten years, no one would doubt the wisdom and foresight in setting up and maintaining this division. In addition to the planing officer, who heads the division, there are several education officers, an architect, a clerk of works, a statistician and an executive officer and typist, as usual, and a number of draughtsmen.

The divisions that have been outlined in this brief account, are manned by public servants, who carry the huge task of administering and implementing the nation's development plans for education. They deserve credit for their service. What is proposed to be done is communicated to those at school level by way of circulars or letters or even a directive, or by means of discussion.

Most writers in the Ministry of Education write in the name of the Permanent Secretary. Replies to these letters are also often addressed to the Permanent Secretary although the fact is that once they get into the Ministry they are directed to the people scheduled to deal with the matter being written about. A teacher writing officially to the officials in the Ministry is required by custom to send the letter through his headmaster/headmistress. Provided this procedure has been observed, he/ she will get a reply which will also be sent through the headmaster's office.

A teacher wishing to do so can get expert advice from the Inspectorate concerning, for instance, how to teach a certain aspect of the syllabus or what materials to use. Heads, too, can get the Inspectorate to make arrangements to come and give assistance to any teachers whom they think needs it. The point being made here is that the Ministry is organised in such away that there is no problem in getting assistance on professional and administrative matters, if so desired.

Every year the Ministry of Education publishes a report on its activities and a summary of achievements. Reports, which should be read by every teacher, highlight the size of the task of administration of education. The details of the reports clearly indicate the high degree to which the staff at the Ministry has been organised to handle all aspects of education. Decisions are made, expansion and consolidation planned, and, particularly through the Inspectorate, professional advice is given. There is also evidence that every effort is made to make the system effectively productive and that the system keeps abreast with current developments in teaching.

Inspection

Why Inspect Schools?
The simple answer to this question is: In order to examine and evaluate a school as a place of learning so that advice and guidance may be given verbally and in writing concerning improvement. The objective of inspection is the raising of educational standards in schools. Recent Education Acts, as we indicate later in this account, have tended to stress the school Inspector's administrative role and have said little or nothing about his role of keeping teachers in touch with pedagogic developments.

The powers of an Inspector of Schools
The Uganda Education Act 1970 has this to say:

An Inspector of schools may at any time, with or without notice, enter any school or any place at which it is reasonably suspected that a school is being conducted and
(i) Inspect and report to the Chief Inspector of Schools with respect to the school or any aspect thereof including any building, workshop, dormitory, hostel; kitchens used in connection with the school, and any other building or property on the site of the school;
(ii) Inspect and audit the accounts of the school and may temporarily remove any books or records for the purpose of inspection or audit.

Every headmaster, on being so requested by an inspector of schools, shall place at the disposal of the Inspector of schools all the records, accounts, note-books, and any other material belonging to the school for inspection or audit by the Inspector of schools.

Every person who willfully obstructs an Inspector of schools from lawfully entering or, having entered, from making an inspection of a school or its accounts commits an offence and shall be liable on conviction to a fine not exceeding two thousand shillings.

The Act spells out the powers of an Inspector of schools in no uncertain terms. If you obstruct him from lawfully entering a school for the purpose of inspection, you are liable on conviction to what is obviously a painfully heavy fine. The Act does not define inspection. Nor does it define an Inspector. It does not dispel from the minds of many headmasters and teachers the image of an Inspector as part detective, part-accountant, or a visitor to be received with nothing more than formal courtesy. Professor A. Wandira has related a recent incident which amply illustrates the image schools and school operators have of the Inspector. Professor Wandira writes:

"I decided to make an unannounced stop at a primary school. I stopped my car several yards from the School for fear that the car-engine might disturb classes then going on. There were several groups of children undertaking what appeared to be outdoor activity. Within a few minutes of my arrival, the Headmaster emerged and with great courtesy showed me to his office, inviting me to say whether I wanted to see the school register of attendance and records. Meanwhile, the groups of children I had found outside disappeared behind doors and the school was frozen into silence. When I confessed that I was no inspector of schools the Headmaster burst into smiles."

Forms of Inspection in Uganda
In the last six years, inspection for Secondary Schools has tended to follow the pattern here briefly described.

Full Inspection
First, there is what is called 'full Inspection.' A month or two before a full inspection takes place, the C.I.S. or a Senior Inspector acting on his behalf advises the Headmaster/Headmistress of the impending inspection. With the notice is usually a request for information about the school. For school inspection in 1971, for instance, the Inspectors required information on something like twenty-two items sent at least a week before the commencement of inspection. There is a number of things expected of each teacher when visited by an Inspector of Schools. Each teacher should be able to offer right away the following:

(i) A scheme of work for the whole department.
(ii) A personal scheme of work for the classes taught.
(iii) A forecast and record of work term by term.
(iv) A record of prep which has been set.
(v) A record of marks.

There must be evidence of appropriate exercises properly marked. All teachers when on duty are expected to be clean, neatly dressed and tidy in appearance.

Heads of Department, in addition to all the requirements we have mentioned, are expected to be able to convey to the Inspectors their control over the direction and organisation of their department with special reference to schemes of work, records of work, allocation of lessons, textbooks, teaching methods, public examination syllabuses and records of stocks equipment. Inspectors will also seek evidence of a teacher's participation in matters of discipline and organisation of the school's extra-curricular activities.

A full inspection lasts from three to five days. The first part of the first day is usually spent with the headteacher who gives as much general information about the school as possible. He answers questions Inspectors may wish to ask. After this meeting, Inspectors see teachers at work, talk to students, take part in Assembly and visit the whole school – some will eat a school meal. Before the end of the inspection each member of the panel calls on the headteacher and discusses positively and constructively the teaching he has seen. On the last day the whole panel has a long session with the Chairman of the school's Board of Governors and the headteacher to discuss the school's problems and consider suggestions for improvement which the inspectors may care to make.

The full inspection is followed by a confidential report. It is not available to staff but the headteacher may at his discretion read out to a member of staff a section which concerns him/her. General criticism may be brought to the notice of the staff for reaction.

2.   Pastoral or Advisory Inspection
The Inspector now comes as adviser and colleague to the classroom teacher. This type of inspection, unavoidably, often exposes the strength or weakness of an Inspector; for to advise the Inspector must be a specialist of the subject and

adequately experienced in teaching it and conversant with current innovations in its teaching. He/ she must have something positive to offer. No reports are made after the inspection.

3. Partial Inspection

This is undertaken at the request of the headteacher or Board of Governors. The partial inspection may be to discipline a teacher who is negligent of his/ her classroom duties or the purpose may be to obtain an impartial professional assessment of a teacher's performance, useful in deciding whether to terminate his/ her service or keep him/ her. The teacher in question is warned in ample time to prepare for inspection.

How does one become an Inspector of schools?

The Uganda Education Act 1970 has an extremely simplified answer to this question. The Act simply says: The Chief Education Officer by notice, may publish in the gazette, appoint any public officer to be an Inspector of Schools.' Surely, not any public officer, otherwise there would be no problem of understaffing – for as previously mentioned, the Inspectorate is understaffed at the moment. Normally, qualifications required of a subject inspector, for instance, are a good degree, at least five years' experience as a competent classroom teacher and considerable degree of professional maturity. It is extremely embarrassing to find that an inspector has given those he/ she is inspecting ground to suspect his/ her knowledge of the subject he/ she is inspecting is inadequate and that he/ she has virtually nothing to offer by way of guidance. It is hoped in this connection that the Faculty of Education at Makerere University in the near future will run courses to prepare Inspectors of schools. For, you see, we now need Inspectors that teachers at school level will respect and whose advice they would be anxious to seek. We need an Inspector so adequately equipped that he/ she is responsive to the advance of knowledge in his/ her field of specialisation, to changes in professional thinking, to innovation and current experiments in education. We need an Inspector who is well ahead of the classroom teacher in embracing new ideas, in discovering sources and types of information useful in connection with teaching problems. For instance, for science we need an Inspector who will encourage teachers to employ methods which would enable students to achieve an understanding of the techniques and underlying principles of science.

Administration at District level - A brief note

When in 1964 the Government had the posts of Mission Schools Supervisors abolished, the work of administration of education services was centralised in what, in those days, were known as Area Education Offices. Each office was manned by an Officer, in some places styled Divisional Education Officer and in some places District Education Officer, with the assistance of Assistant Education Officers. The number of Assistant Education Officers would depend on the needs, the size, and the number of schools in the District. The main reason for the Government's move, as already mentioned, was to effect integration of schools, to economise on resources, and to eliminate duplication of services. Prior to the changes of 1964, it will be recalled that the Chief Education Officer, Ministry of Education Kampala handed grants for post-primary institutions to Education Secretaries General; the Provincial Education Officers of Eastern, Northern, Western and Buganda Regions passed grants to Education Secretaries for Junior Secondary Schools; District Education Officers passed grants to School Supervisors. The office of Provincial Education Officer was re-named Regional Inspector and the duties changed with the changes of 1964. The District Education Officer was given more duties and more powers exercisable under the surveillance of the Chief Education Officer.

Today, the key man in the administration of educational service concerned with Primary Schools in a District is the District Education Officer or D.E.O. as often referred to. His duties can be summarised as follows:

He acts as Secretary of the Education Committee and he is its professional adviser. He prepares the annual estimates of the District's Education Committee and takes executive action on its decisions. He advises the Management Committee and interprets Government policy to it. His office is a resource center for teaching materials for use in Primary Schools. He advises primary head teachers on matters concerning timetables and syllabuses. With the assistance of one or two Assistant Inspectors of schools attached to his office, he arranges for the inspection of Primary Schools, runs refresher courses, and recommends teachers for upgrading courses. He further arranges for the payment of grants for school buildings, equipment and furniture, and salaries to primary teachers. He is responsible for the proper collection of school fees and handles head teachers' requisitions for money for running certain services in the schools as prescribed by the authorities.

The District Education Officer is further responsible, in the last analysis, for the discipline of the teachers and of the pupils. He, on behalf of the Chief Education Officer, makes arrangements for the transfer of teachers and is responsible for seeing to it that the distribution of teachers for Primary Schools in his district is fair and balanced. He reminds teachers of the requirements of the Teachers' Conditions of Service. It should be noted that provision has been made normally for a number of subcommittees of the Education Committee to help with the administration of educational services. The three of these are: the Bursary Committee, Finance Committee, and the General Purposes Committee.

One of the problems of administration of education services at District level is that the Districts are mainly geographical districts. Hence, the D.E.O. often has a large number of Primary Schools under his charge separated by long distances, a factor which strains the material and human resources at the disposal of the D.E.O. Again, the D.E.O. has to try and cope with problems of expansion of Primary School facilities in his District, so that more and more children can be absorbed into school.

To conclude, it is important to point out that the D.E.O.'s office is expected to keep, and keeps, records and is expected to furnish the Ministry with statistics on aspects of education in the District.

The legal framework of education

None of the three Sovereign States of E.A. has compulsory school attendance laws yet. Each, however, has made laws, i.e. rules and arrangements recognised by the courts, for effective control and supervision of all schools maintained by public funds and even those maintained by private funds.

In Uganda, the Education Act 1970 has amended and consolidated the law relating to the development and regulation of education, the registration and licensing of teachers in public and private schools, and for other matters connected therein. It should be noted that the Minister may by statutory order declare any school or college to be exempt from the application of the Act.

In Kenya, the Education Act 1968 has charged the Minister of Education with the duty of promoting the education of Kenyans and the progressive development of institutions concerned with education. It is the Minister's responsibility to formulate a development plan for education in Kenya.

In Uganda, the already mentioned Education Officer prescribes the appointment of a Chief Education, a Chief Inspector of Schools, Inspectors of schools, and Education Officers. All Education Officers and Inspectors are under the direction of the C.E.O.; Inspectors are authorised to enter any school at any time, with or without notice, to find out what is going on. The law requires operators of a school to put at the disposal of the Inspector all records and accounts and prescribes severe penalty for refusal to do so.

Answers to two questions, for example, illustrate the extent to which the law has gone to bring all education under the control of the authorities.

(a) It is a fact that because of well-known circumstances, the authorities cannot provide schools for all children. Can any person establish a private school? Yes, if a number of conditions are satisfied:

(i) He should apply to the C.E.O. to be approved as a suitable person to establish a private school and have the necessary funds to manage the school he proposes to start.
(ii) He must get the Ministry to confirm that the proposed school will form part of the education development plan prepared for the area by the Ministry.
(iii) He must get the Ministry to confirm that the proposed school will meet the educational needs of that area.
(iv) His application should be supported by at least three persons of good standing in the area.

If these conditions are fully satisfied and the application is approved, the prospective school owner cannot get permission to operate his school until seven other conditions are fulfilled.

(i) The Ministry of Education must have approved all building plans.
(ii) Appropriate authority must have inspected completed buildings.
(iii) There must be adequate provision of staff housing where necessary.
(iv) He must undertake to engage a headmaster whom the C.E.O. regards as suitable for the type of school proposed.
(v) He is required to satisfy the C.E.O. that prospective teachers are eligible to teach in the school he proposes to open, and that the school will have facilities adequate for the type of school he intends it to be.
(vi) He must indicate vividly that the physical health and moral welfare of the students will be properly provided for.
(vii) He must undertake that admission will be open to all. Permission to operate the school is provisional and is for one year; after which period the owner applies to C.E.O. to have the school classified and registered provided it is, in the opinion of C.E.O., properly run and organised. The Act empowers the C.E.O. to cancel the registration of a private school if it contravenes the Act.

Any person who decides to establish a school and act as if the Law did not exist is liable on conviction to a fine of 6,000/=.

(b) It is a fact there is a great shortage of teachers. Can anyone who feels like doing so teach in any public or private schools?

The answer is 'No'. The Law says: 'No person shall teach in any public or private school of any description unless he is registered as a teacher. Persons who apply to be registered must meet two conditions:
(i) They must have successfully completed a teacher education course approved by the Ministry.
(ii) They must have applied to the C.E.O. for registration in the manner prescribed by C.E.O.

The Uganda Education Act 1970 requires school owners to manage them in such a way that the interests of the pupils are supreme. The Minister is empowered to prescribe fees. There is also provision for the Minister of Education to make regulations, prescribing the course of instruction and the examinations to be taken after such a course and governing the suspension, exclusion or expulsion of pupils from attending school.

The teacher and the law

As a citizen, the teacher is affected by law as other citizens are. Breach of law by the teacher would cause him to face court action and its possible consequences. Other citizens aggrieved, injured, or whose names are brought into dispute by his actions, may and can sue the teacher in a court of law. Criminal and civil proceedings may and can be taken against the teacher if there are grounds for doing so. Parents, pupils and even his employers may and can, if there are grounds for doing so, take a teacher to court to show cause why. Teachers, too, can and may sue any of the parties mentioned above if there is cause.

However, we are concerned here with the teacher and the law that has been made to regulate or guide the behaviour of those who teach in schools, be they private or public. First of all, the question as to who employs the teacher over which there was a tangle of confusion from the 1940s to 1961 does not arise now. All teachers are Government employees or public servants unless they work in private independent schools. The law, therefore, which affects them is the law made by the Authorities and enforceable by means as prescribed by the Government. Each teacher is required by law (to be specific, by the Education Act, 1970), to be registered in the manner prescribed in the Act. There is also provision for issuing a statement of eligibility by the C.E.O., on payment of a prescribed fee, which entitles someone who has not undergone training as a teacher to be enrolled as a licensed teacher and to be given a licence to teach for a maximum of two years. The validity of the statement of eligibility is two years but is renewable. The C.E.O. is empowered by law to endorse on a licence the level at which the holder can teach or the subject he is allowed to teach. There is no need at all to go into detailed explanation why teachers should be registered or alternatively licensed. The fact is that for practitioners of all professions registration is mandatory and there are conditions which must be fully met before one can be enrolled.

As a worker and as a an employee of the Ministry of Education, the teacher is subject to and is required to observe rules recognised by courts of law and known as 'Teachers Conditions of Service 1962'. Until they are revised or cancelled, any teacher in the service who conducts himself as if the rules did not exist, does so at the risk of facing punishment, consequent upon proceedings brought under the provision of the rules.

The rules lay down:
(i) Teacher's duties – requiring each teacher to devote such time to his duties as is made necessary by their nature.
(ii) That a new teacher serves a two year probationary period.

For example, the law says:
(i) A teacher shall normally be required to serve for a continuous period of two years on probation before being confirmed in the permanent service.
Provided that the Chief Education Officer may, at his discretion, extend the period of probation by not more than one year.
(ii) Upon satisfactorily completing a probationary period a teacher shall be confirmed by the Chief Education Officer with effect from the date of his first appointment.
(iii) If at any time during his probationary period it appears to the Chief Education Officer that a teacher is unlikely to merit confirmation, then he shall inform such teacher in writing of this fact, setting out the reasons therefore.

(a) if a teacher is certified unfit, then he shall be discharged;
(b) if in the opinion of the medical officer conducting the examination such teacher would be fit after a course of treatment, the Chief Education Officer may extend the probationary period to allow such treatment as is necessary to be taken;
(c) in cases of doubt, a second medical opinion may be obtained with the approval of the service committee or service sub-committee, as the case may be.

The law (rules) has a lot to say about salary. The most attractive and noticeable aspect is that salary shall be paid in twelve equal instalments. According to the rules, when a teacher travels to a school on his first appointment, his reasonable travel expenses should be paid by the school to which he has been appointed.

The rules relate also to sick leave and maternity leave. Notice carefully that a teacher who is absent from duty owing to sickness for a period of two days or more may be required by the headmaster to produce a medical certificate signed by a medical officer justifying his absence.

There are subjects the rules relate to which deserve special attention.

Termination of appointment
On this the law says:
(i) A teacher in the permanent service shall not be discharged without due notice, i.e. 2 Calendar months prior to April 30th, August 31st and December 31st or salary instead of this notice.
(ii) A teacher must give due notice when resigning or alternatively obtain C.E.O's consent to leave without due notice.
(iii) Any teacher who fails to give due notice or obtain C.E.O's consent, shall according to the rules be dismissed.

Misconduct and inefficiency
(i) Absence: unauthorised absence calls for loss of salary for the period of absence.
(ii) Concerning misconduct and inefficiency the law says: Whenever it comes to the knowledge of a headmaster, education officer or management committee that a teacher has been guilty of misconduct or inefficiency or an inspector has reported adversely on a teacher, the headmaster, education officer, or management committee, as the case may be, shall in writing report such misconduct or inefficiency or adverse report through the Education Officer, as the case may be, to the Teaching Service Commission or Service Commission or Service Sub-committee, as the case may be.

When a report is made under the provision of the preceeding sub-rule:
(a) the headmaster, education officer, or sub-committee, as the case may be, shall inform the teacher concerned in writing that such a report has been made, giving reasons for the report;

(b) the education officer, may at the same, suspend the teacher from duty until such time as the committee has determined what action should be taken on the report.
(c) the teacher shall have the right to appear before the committee personally or to make written representation to such committee, in respect of the matter reported.
(d) In any case in which the committee considers a medical examination to be necessary, the teacher concerned may be required to undergo such examination.

If any teacher is arrested upon a criminal charge involving moral turpitude, he shall be suspended from duty with effect from the date of his arrest and the Education Officer shall forthwith report the fact to the service committee or Service Sub-committee, as the case may be.

(iii) The law further says:

Any teacher who:
(a) conducts himself in a manner which interferes with the efficient conduct of the school; or
(b) uses for purposes unconnected with the service, confidential information which he obtained in the course of his duties; or
(c) without the knowledge and permission of the Chief Education Officer, accepts directly or indirectly, any gratuity present or reward from any member of the public in respect of anything done by him in the discharge of his duties; or
(d) is dishonest or insolent in the course of his duties; or
(e) is negligent or lazy in the performance of his duties; or
(f) renders himself unfit for duty by the use of intoxicating liquor or drugs; or
(g) is guilty of immoral conduct; or
(h) does anything which is likely to bring the Service into disrepute; or
(i) uses his position as a teacher to encourage disrespect for or disobedience to government or any laws or order; or
(j) uses his position as a teacher to further the views of any political party or to expound his own political views; or
(k) knowingly contravenes the provisions of the ordinance; or
(e) is convicted in a court of law on charges involving moral turpitude, shall be guilty of misconduct and may be punished under the provisions of the Rules, by the Chief Education Officer, Service Committee or Service Sub-committee, as the case may be.

(iv) Penalties are indicated as follows:
(a) Dismissal – termination of teacher's appointment without due notice.
(b) Discharge-appointment is terminated with due notice.
(c) Withholding of increment.

(d) Temporary reduction of salary
(e) Permanent reduction of salary
(f) Reprimand

The rules provide for appeal by the aggrieved teacher to the Teaching Service Commission.

7

Administration: School level (secondary)

Board of Governors

For each school, which is financed according to current provision by the Government, there is by law a Board of Governors. The origin of Board of Governors dates back to 1944 when under the Self-Governing School Rules, Boards of Governors were appointed for six Secondary Schools and two Training Colleges under the management of voluntary agencies. After that, every year, the Government encouraged the main institutions to have boards so that by 1960 nearly all Secondary Schools, Teacher Training Colleges and Technical Institutions had boards

In 1962 under the provision of the 1959 Education Ordinance, section 33, under legal notice number 129 of 1962, The Board of Governors (Self-Governing Schools) Rules 1962 were published. Up to the time of writing this account, boards have operated and have been set up as the rules direct. Each Board of Governors consists of 13 members. The Minister of Education must approve membership of the Board. Members of School Boards do not receive any salary or allowance for their services. We gather that with the operation of the Education Act 1970, the Board of Governors rules may be revised. As you may have seen when reading the Act, the Minister may by regulations make provision, inter alia, for allowances to be paid to the members.

But whether we take them as constituted now or as they will be constituted under the new Act, School Boards of Governors are responsible for the administration and for the proper and efficient conduct of schools under their charge. A school Board of Governors is given responsibility of exercising supervisory control of the headmaster/headmistress and all teaching and non-teaching staff to an extent determined by the Ministry. Unfortunately, the Board of Governors Rules in force at the time of writing this account do not define the duties and responsibilities of Board Members clearly and precisely. Added to this, is the disturbing fact that too frequently the only contact the majority of members have with the school is when they attend Board Meetings and meet the headmaster and, perhaps, his deputy, hardly ever meeting teaching members of staff or even a single student. Although the rules require at least two meetings a year, some Boards meet once a year; it is not uncommon for meetings to be cancelled for lack of a quorum because some members have either been transferred to other parts of the country and, therefore, cannot travel the long distance to come to meeting, or they are too busy to come.

Furthermore, although the rules are at least clear as far as responsibilities of the headmaster are concerned, some of their requirements are no longer complied with. For instance, the Headmaster is required 'to arrange the academic curriculum and syllabus (Paragraph 13) of the School, having due regard to the general instructions of the Board and advice of the Chief Inspector of Schools.' The reality is that curriculum and syllabus are determined by the Ministry and there is no room for the general instructions of the Board. (Some Board members are not educationist – how could they issue instructions concerning curriculum?).

Furthermore, there are other matters affecting the school, for example, staffing, admission of pupils, reporting on staff (confidential reports), receipt of money grants for the school – for which the headmaster deals directly with the Ministry of Education without going through the Board. In most cases, he simply informs them what has happened. The Boards, consequently, are not as strong as they might be.

However, despite all this, and despite the lack of a clear and precise definition of the Boards' responsibilities and duties, it is customarily known now that each Board is required to perform the following duties:

(i) The Board, before the end of each school year, must study carefully the school's audited accounts of the preceding year and the report thereon, and, in the light of this exercise, advise the headmaster on matters such as control of expenditure if there are grounds to suggest that expenditure has not been controlled. In recent years, a number of school boards with concern have noticed the rising costs of running Secondary Schools and have duly reported the situation to the authorities. Boards of Governors take very seriously the mismanagement of the school's finance and their concern is recorded in the minutes of their meeting, a copy of which must be sent to the Ministry of Education.

(ii) The Board must approve the headmaster's proposed estimates of expenditure of the school's income for the coming school year, i.e. 1 January to 31 December. It is after the Board has approved the estimates that the headmaster may send a copy to the Ministry of Education for final approval.

(iii) The Board has to decide, if occasion arises, whether a student should be expelled from the school under them.

(iv) The Board must study the School Inspection report and cause action to be taken in the light of the Inspector's recommendations and advice.

(v) In the event of disruption at school, the Board is expected to meet without delay to see how to deal with the situation. As already mentioned, the Education Act 1970 indicates that by regulations the Minister of Education may make provision for Boards of Governors concerning, inter alia, their powers in relation to the headmaster, staff of the school, funds of the school, and the procedure at board meetings. In recent years, some Boards have been very active and displayed initiative but the number of these is not large. No Board, however strong, does or can do the actual day-to-day administration of a given school.

Who does the actual day-to-day administration of a school?

Who does the administration of the school? It is not adequate to answer this question simply by saying that it is the headteacher. Administration of a given school (Secondary Schools particularly) embodies all that is done at school to try and satisfy pupils' needs. Pupils' needs are obvious – good teaching; good food; good conditions for work, study and sleep, for athletics, sports and games; opportunities for co-curricular activities, particularly social activities such as dancing, both traditional and foreign; music; contacts with the community in terms of service to it or from it as deemed most desirable; and supervised contact with other schools.

In addition to these needs, there are the less obvious, emotional and human needs. All pupils need understanding, consideration, a feeling that the headteacher and staff are with them. But we must caution teachers willingly subscribing to the proposition that staff members are servants of the pupils. We think that this may be dangerous as it is likely to breed youthful arrogance and scorn of authority.

All the teachers and the headteacher (who is a teacher, too) should fully and sincerely participate in the administration of the school. The administration of the school will collapse sooner or later and a 'strike' or some other kind of rebellion by students may take place if teachers, however small the number may be, do not participate fully. A teacher who constantly comes late to class, a teacher who does not prepare his/ her lessons, a teacher who sets no work or when he/ she sets it does not mark it, a teacher who says to pupils 'however much you may try you will not pass', should not claim to be contributing to the administration of the school in the light of the definition of school administration given here.

When a teacher finishes the teacher training and goes to school to start work, the headmaster or the headmistress at once involves him/ her in the administration of the school. He will not give him a wide range of duties. Besides teaching in the classroom, where performance will be expected to be of a very high standard, he may be asked to be food master, take charge of sports, take interest in student societies, advise a school magazine committee, help pupils in organizing their weekend entertainment, accompany football teams even if he himself has never kicked a ball. The headmaster may put him in charge of a class of 40 pupils or a dormitory of 180 pupils and he will be expected to devote time to the welfare of these pupils; he must get to know them. He must see to it that their dormitory is clean. If he is in charge of a dormitory, it is obligatory that he lives on the campus. His ideas will be invited on a number of school problems. Pupils will take their problems to him; some he will certainly solve; others may give him headaches. Incidentally, a good teacher may find himself doing things on his own initiative and this will be appreciated.

It could be argued that after a reasonably conscientious man or woman has taught, for say, a full academic school year in a school, it is not correct to say that he has no experience in school administration. Some people, because of their erroneous and narrow definition of school administration, associate experience of school administration with people who have worked as deputy headmasters or as acting headmasters. Even people who should know make utterances which wrongly suggest the administration of the school includes only what the head and his deputy do. At a staff meeting at School X the head told his staff, 'your job is in the classroom, your job is to teach and to do nothing but teach, leave the administration of the school to me.' He was wrong.

Although we know there are certain great responsibilities which the headmaster shoulders, he couldn't possibly carry out a single one of them without being assisted by the work the staff does. For many years, people believed that special men or women were needed to be heads of Secondary Schools. It is hard to agree with E..B. Castle the author of Growing up in East Africa, written in 1966, in which he talked about the scarcity of Africans of headmasters calibre, and even urged the need for a ''secret staff college to provide training and experience both at home and abroad' to fit the selected few for headmastership.' A practicing teacher working in a school where there is opportunity to participate fully in the administration of the school, and we repeat, as we have defined it, does not need special training and experience 'both at home and abroad' to be made headmaster.

Some problems of secondary school administration

In the last six or so years, what have been called strikes have occurred in a number of our schools. Indeed, very few big Secondary Schools have not known a strike. The word strike is a misnomer as far as student protests are concerned; for a strike is the withholding of paid labour and indeed, under certain conditions, it is a lawful form of action that can be successfully used to obtain redress. During a school strike, students are not withholding any kind of paid labour. Rather, they are in fact denying themselves a service for which their parents have paid directly via fees, and indirectly through taxes.

During school strike, students have rejected normal rules of conduct, have boycotted one or more routine activities such as lessons, students have stoned buildings and teachers, tipped staff cars, and on several occasions headmasters' cars were set on fire. The frequency of strikes and the violence and vandalism associated with them have made a lot of people, and teachers included, consider indiscipline as the major problem of school administration in this country. There was indeed a time when it appeared as if indiscipline was becoming a problem that baffled school administrators. School administration is no longer worried about strikes. With experience and devices now used to involve students more and more in certain aspects of school administration, it is possible to avoid the indiscipline and upheaval which beset schools several years ago.

It is also suggested here that each teacher should from the start explain carefully to the pupils that no school can provide ideal conditions for living and learning, pointing out problems Uganda is facing and the big effort being made by the Government to solve them. It is important that explanation be backed up with information on say, actual costs of food, teaching materials, the pressures and problems faced by the staff. Whenever he can, the teacher should spend some time in discussing the structure of the school as a society within which an individual, from the humblest domestic worker to the senior teachers, has certain rights and privileges which certainly involve obligations. There are, obviously, obligations which each member of the school society owes to any other member, pupil to teacher, teacher to pupil, all of them to the school. Each teacher has the duty to keep himself informed about the school. He should endeavour to help pupils to overcome their difficulties.

Large enrolments: Incidentally, we are using the word problem to convey the same meaning as challenge. In response to the need for secondary education on the part of many Ugandans, a number of things have been done. One of these is the raising of the number of pupils per stream from 25 to 40. In dormitories, double-deck beds are used. The number per stream apart, the number of streams per class is now in most schools at least three. Some schools run double sessions i.e. half the school in the morning and half the school in the afternoon.

But what the school population explosion means as far as school administration is concerned, is this, that every teacher has to organise himself and help organise the pupils at a pace and to a pattern in accordance with changing circumstances. Assignments must be given and assessed. Every effort must be made to call pupils by their right names and interest shown in them as individuals.

School Finance

A secondary School has two sources of income: (a) school fees – rates are not uniform; they vary from school to school: (b) capitation grants, 840 E.A. Shs – H.S.C. boarding 420 E.A. Shs Day, 472 E.A. Shs-S1-4 boarding and 210 E.A. Shs. S1-4 day. What is collected from these two sources is used to cover a wide range of expenses that must be incurred in running a school for the whole year. While a school can be certain of capitation grants, which are paid by the Government, it can never tell how successful it will be as far as collecting all fees in a given year is concerned. With the present inflation, it is not at all easy to operate a school. Many of the students, as many teachers discover, just do not understand when you say the school has no money for things outside essentials. All teachers are often asked to accept drastic economics, and to see to it there is no deliberate waste of teaching materials and damage to school property by students. Lack of money for certain things that may be needed, is, and should be, the concern of every member of the school community. Students will often ask why the headmaster doesn't call on the Ministry for more funds. Of course, the Ministry is asked, and the Ministry does, when it is in position to do so, supply .funds apart from capitation grant for providing facilities that become necessary in the course of expansion, for example, or on introduction of new courses.

All personnel working in a school have a responsibility to explain to pupils of all levels that, in the present circumstances, there is a number of things a school can do without and still carry on effectively. Buses and fleets of vans for example, a school can do without.

Teachers' salaries are paid by the Ministry, except for the expatriate staff; money for paying teachers' salaries is sent to the school each month and, therefore, no head can say he has no money to pay salaries. Incidentally, contrary to what some people think, the salaries are good. There is also provision for paying responsibility allowances in some areas, clearly and generously defined.

Some devices used in school administration

When the school community is a happy one, its administration does not pose very many problems. Building a happy school community is the aim of every headmaster. Much of the success in this area depends on pupil-staff relationship and good personal relationships. A new staff member will find stress being put on his being readily approachable by pupils and he will be asked to recognise and respect this right. If for instance, in a boarding school he is made a housemaster, he should visit students, talk with them, help them with their activities, smooth over their difficulties. In other words, try and break down the barrier that so often exists across the classroom desk. It is often outside the classroom that the desk barrier can first be broken. Keeping pupils at a distance may not produce respect which is born of mutual understanding and trust. No one will ask you to be unduly familiar because a pupil does not expect a teacher to be his equal, but avoid being aloof. Many heads reasonably emphasise the importance of example as no pupil can respect a teacher whose behaviour is reprehensible. We mention here some of the devices used for effective school administration:

Staff meetings

These days, for effective school administration, emphasis is placed on channels of communication. Many schools have regular staff meetings at which normally the head will ensure that every teacher has opportunity to air views. It is at such meetings that staff differences will or should be thrashed out. Under no circumstances, as far as we can see, should a teacher express his views to the pupils in opposition to the policy of the school as laid down, for instance, by the headmaster or as agreed by the majority (and this does not need to be a sweeping majority) of the staff. Staff meetings which are basically the business meeting of the staff discuss the whole field of school affairs, curriculum change implementation, teaching methods, and discipline. They have a considerable degree of formality, have an agenda, and their minutes are kept. In addition to general staff meetings, it is not unusual for staff of a department to meet for business concerning their department.

Prefects
All Uganda schools now have a prefect system, and prefects are selected and appointed in the manner prescribed by the Ministry of Education. The precis of a detailed procedure is that prefects are appointed by the head and staff from a list of pupils nominated as prescribed for the post of prefect, by the pupils themselves. Prefects participate in school administration.

School councils or parliaments, as the press sometimes refers to them
Since the beginning of 1970, each school (Secondary School) is required to have a school council composed of prefects and other pupils elected by a class or by a house in a manner prescribed by the Ministry of Education. The prefects and the school council members are generally representatives of the pupils and are an indication of the place now accorded to the pupils as far as school administration is concerned. The two bodies separately or jointly act as a channel of communication between pupils and school authorities and call the attention of the head and his staff to problems that they may not have noticed because of pressure of work or even indifference. The two bodies now, in some schools, administer a number of school pupil services on their own initiative and without supervision by staff.

Assembly
Many schools use this device as means of communicating to the school when it is gathered together in one place at the same time. It is already becoming difficult to use the assembly because of numbers – where can you meet? In some schools a teacher may be called upon to communicate to the pupils what would have been said at the assembly.

What about punishment, expulsion and school rules?
There are two or three things connected with school administration which many people talk about, both inside and outside the school. The first of these is the

subject of punishments. Reluctantly, we have to admit the necessity for punishment in school as a corrective. But we, like many school administrators and educators, emphasise patience and the necessity for careful consideration of every case. You will find that many Secondary School pupils are very sensitive to injustice. Good school administration now avoids mass punishments as much as possible. It is now a practice to ask teachers to avoid putting themselves in an untenable position by making threats. Warning that such and such an act is wrong is often sufficient. If punishment is to be administered, it must be made clear that there are sufficient grounds for it; if this were not the case and the pupil refused to do it problems would arise. Corporal punishment is out of place in Secondary Schools, for obvious reasons.

Expulsions

Many questions are raised in connection with this subject. For what offences should a pupil be expelled from school? Should a pupil expelled from one school be accepted by another school in the system? If a pupil, the son of a tax payer, is expelled from one school, doesn't the expelling school have a duty to help the pupil in question get into another school? Doesn't expulsion contribute to wastage which, considering manpower requirements, we ought to avoid? We will not attempt to answer these questions; all we can safely say here is what is done now when circumstances arise in which it becomes necessary to consider the removal of the impossible pupil from school.

The headmaster has the authority to order any pupil, whose continued presence in the school is considered detrimental to the school at that time, to leave and return home pending the consideration of his case by the Board of Governors. The term used for this kind of action is 'indefinite suspension'. The Board in consultation with the C.E.O. can decide expulsion of a student.

School Rules

The second thing connected with school administration is the subject of school rules. The current trend is to avoid a multiplicity of rules which would be very difficult to remember and to enforce and which would cause irritation on the part of pupils. There has been a suggestion that the Ministry of Education should issue a set of uniform rules with prescribed punishments, for use in schools. This kind of suggestion must be rejected as totally unsuitable and impracticable. Reasons? No two schools are alike, and the whole essence of a code of rules is that it must fit the circumstances and objectives of the community for which it is designed. A rule that cannot be enforced is valueless. There are perhaps grounds for the Ministry to give some general guide lines to school administrators on how to deal with major disciplinary problems – for example, drink, stealing and sexual misconduct. But as you can see all these are moral problems; therefore, when dealing with them difficulties do arise.

The Administration of certain services

1. School finance

Before the end of each school year, the headmaster is required to lay before the school's Board of Governors proposals for expenditure or estimates and notes thereon for the coming school year for discussion. As already mentioned, the school's income as derived from capitation grants and fees collected from students, is divided among a long list of items that call for expenditure of money in the course of the year for administering the school. Proposals are submitted on a form prescribed by the Ministry of Education. The form has two sections, first, estimated income and, second, estimated recurrent expenditure on items prescribed by the Ministry of Education. At the time of writing, the form used has 46 items for proposed expenditure.

Unlike heads of Departments in the Civil Service who estimate expenditure and get the money granted if estimates are regarded as justifiable by Treasury, what the headmaster does is to divide up the limited income expected among the items of expenditure. We very much doubt whether, in the last three years particularly, any headmaster has presented to his Board of Governors estimates that represented the actual expenditure when the year in question came. With static income, circumstances of rising costs have made the drawing up of estimates a real headache. There is a tendency in many schools to make relatively generous allocations only to those items which must be supplied, otherwise students become restive or the morale of both teachers and students is dampened. Items such as food, fuel, lighting, water, get considerable attention. Items for which there was no money and the headmaster would be listened to, get least attention.

Boards of Governors study estimates carefully, item by item, asking questions for clarification, but in the experience of the authors, do not really have anything to suggest except that they express the wish that school had more money on such and such items. The situation, as it is, calls for an up-grading revision of rates of capitation grants or, if possible, substantial rise in fees (this is impossible). Boarding Schools in particular are in financial straits (1970 – 71).

After the estimates have been seen by the Board of Governors, they are submitted to the Ministry of Education.

Financial administration at school-current practices

Every Secondary School must have a Bursar who is concerned with the school's accounts. In the majority of schools he receives and issues receipts for fees from pupils. He receives and checks carefully bills from traders before he submits them to the headmaster for approval before payment. On the authority of the headmaster, he pays wages and cash to persons authorised to receive it. He keeps records of all financial transactions in the books and, in the manner prescribed by the Ministry or the Board of Governors, based on the advice of the auditors. He, on the authority of the head, banks school money and takes charge of the safe. He prepares trial balances and must have ready all documents required by auditors for audit purposes. The school Bursar is a key man in the administration of the school's finance; all is well if he is competent and has integrity. However, no matter how good and competent the Bursar may be, the responsibility for the administration of school funds rests squarely on the shoulders of the headmaster. It is the view of the authors that at Faculty of Education, at least, short courses in reading and understanding things like trial balances, balance sheets, and elementary book keeping should be run for newly appointed heads of schools.

Control of expenditure
Success in this area, in many ways, depends obviously on the item in question, how dispensable it is for instance, and how easily available. It also depends on how easily and quickly up-to-date information on expenditure can be obtained from the Bursar. It further depends on the willingness of staff to avoid incurring unnecessary expenses and also on getting pupils to recognise the fact that financial resources of the school are severely limited. Occasionally, a solitary headmaster claims to have kept within his budget and even to have made reserves. This is wonderful, provided it does not mean laboratories without equipment, lack of up-to-date text books, and buildings not properly maintained.

Insurance
Until fairly recently school administration here appears to have thought there were no risks in running a school. Motor vehicles were insured by law and there was no choice. Several cases where schools have been faced with liability suits against them for negligence of their employees (head-teachers) and the occurrence of burglary and robbery of school funds, have caused most schools nowadays to take out insurance policies. A number of schools are insured against:
(i) Workmen's compensation (according to the law the employer, i.e. the school, is liable to pay for compensation for injuries of employees, etc., arising out of and in the course of employment);
(ii) Loss of cash in transit and in the safe;
(iii) Liability to the public
(iv) Burglary and fire

Premiums are considerable and come out of the school's recurrent income. Schools have found it wise to take out insurance policies particularly for items 1, 2 and 4.

Recently, with the encouragement of the Ministry of Education, insurance arrangements have been extended to protect pupils against certain hazards while on the way to and from, and at school if parents pay a moderate premium to an insurance company, which has made its services available.

However, the most important thing is for school administrators, if possible, to avoid imprudent practices which endanger the safety of workmen, students, the public, and the teachers. It pays if headmaster, teachers, and pupils anticipate hazards and accordingly take precautions

Examinations

Some teachers display unacceptable incompetence concerning the administration of examinations. Two parties are involved in examination, the examiner, on one hand and the examinee, on the other. In this country there are two types of examinations, namely internal and external.

Internal examinations

Every teacher participates in these as a setter, marker and assessors of grades. Every teacher would be advised to do the following things:
(i) Decide what the objective of the examination is.
(ii) Set questions at the level of the examinees. For instance, using simple language.
(iii) Draw up a marking scheme and mark in a detailed manner with remarks.
(iv) Record grades and comment on them meaningfully so that, if need be, they can be used to provide some of the basis for reports on the progress of pupils.

External examinations

Teachers are involved in supervision and invigilation. The main external examinations are at present conducted by the East African Examination Council in collaboration with the Cambridge University Examination Syndicate. The examinations are taken at many centers and, indeed, each secondary school is a center and is accordingly given a center number.

Supervisor of centre for external examinations.

The practice used now is to appoint one of the teachers of a school to act as a supervisor of a centre, i.e. to supervise the conduct of external examinations in question. He is responsible for completing examination entry forms and their proper checking and for distributing of timetables. He has to make sure that candidates at the centre are aware of the notices concerning the examinations they are sitting.

He has access to papers and, obviously, this is a great responsibility. He handles scripts, puts them in envelopes as examination regulations require, and sends them in the safest way possible to the Ministry of Education. He is responsible for reporting fully on matters arising in the course of conducting the examinations. He appoints invigilators to assist him.

The duties and responsibilities of the invigilator
(i) To give out stationery to candidates.
(ii) To distribute question papers when the time comes for doing so.
(iii) To collect scripts at the end of the period allocated to the paper in question.
(iv) He has the responsibility of detecting irregular practices and for taking action in the light of the rules of the examination. He must refrain from reading, marking papers and smoking while invigilating.
(v) He has the responsibility of periodically informing candidates how much time remains before they are called upon to stop writing or working.
(vi) He is not expected to leave the room at any time while the examination is still going on.

Supervision

School owners, the Government or otherwise, expect teachers and pupils to be supervised. Teachers supervise pupils on the school premises, including periods of recreation. Each school usually has a system of supervision and every teacher has the responsibility to see to it that it does not break down. In a good number of education systems, the task of supervising the teachers in a given school is assigned to the head teacher. *The dictionary of Education* defines supervision as "All efforts of designated officials directed towards providing leadership to teachers and other educational workers in the improvement of instruction." Out here in East Africa, particularly in the present circumstances, Inspectors of Schools contribute little towards helping teachers to improve instruction. Inspection as designed now, aims mainly at determining whether or not teachers do what they are supposed to do. Questions put to teachers strongly supports this view. Where is the scheme of work? What exercise have you set? How many candidates obtained a credit in your subject in last year's School Certificate Exams? How much of the syllabus have you covered? May we see your preparation book? Inspectors ask these questions and if a teacher does not answer as required he has a problem.

Writers on this topic of supervision have suggested what the head teacher may do in order to supervise his staff.
(i) He should visit the teachers to observe them teach. Following the observation of the lesson, there should be a conference between teacher and head where the latter point out errors or commends the former for good teaching.
(ii) He could call group meetings of teachers of a subject or of class to discuss such matters as methods of teaching of the subject in question.
(iii) Hold staff meetings regularly during which the head could ask staff to discuss problems which bear specifically on instruction.

Let us look at the practicability of these 3 supervisory techniques suggested. Classroom visiting – the visitation and subsequent conference should be used in connection with a teacher on probation and straight out of training and that is all. The head teacher couldn't possibly find time to apply it on a large scale. Furthermore, the higher level of preparation attained by teachers make head teacher's classroom visitation unnecessary. If a head teacher visits a class, it must be in order to identify a problem a teacher is struggling with so that he can discuss it in an informed manner. There is a kind of teacher who cannot be helped – to improve through teachers meetings about a particular subject, and the discussion of methods. Usually this is a weak teacher – he needs different special treatment. It may help to send him to a refresher course. It may again help to readjust his teaching load.

The head teacher will often ask the head of department to convene and preside over meetings of subject teachers to discuss methods and problems of teaching the subject in question. A proper head of department, adequately qualified, usually assumes responsibility throughout the school for a subject or group of subjects. He prepares or should prepare the scheme of work for his department, and has the responsibility for ensuring that continuity of teaching is achieved. He advises on the allocation of duties in his department. He is responsible to the head teacher. In some Ugandan schools, we use heads of department as much as possible and all teachers in the department are asked to co-operate with the head. Good heads of department contribute considerably to the smooth running and maintenance of the standard of teaching at a school. A new teacher should expect the head of his department to want to see his lesson preparation book, exam questions he has set, and will find the head glad to give as much assistance as possible towards his becoming a competent classroom teacher.

Some education systems these days use what they call a consultant teacher. The consultant teacher has responsibilities such as advising new teachers (teachers on probation), raising standards in a class, and initiating experimental teaching projects. We do not have consultant teachers in Uganda but it would be useful to have them.

Lastly, staff meetings do not seem to be an effective medium of dealing with problems which bear specially on instruction.
(a) It is difficult to be sure of 100 per cent attendance.
(b) There is a possibility that the most talkative members of staff will dominate the discussion
(c) Most head teachers turn staff meetings into occasions of lecturing staff on good teaching
(d) Invitably the agenda has often many items mainly to do with administrative routine.

In conclusion, we think schools would do well to have consultant teachers to undertake supervision. Consultant teachers would advise, persuade and guide teachers, and follow up and evaluate the recommendations they make. Some head teachers claim that they supervise their staff effectively. What we suppose they mean is that teachers under them report for duty punctually, do not leave school premises during working hours, send a word if unable to come to school, and call the register. This is supervision as exercised by a foreman in a factory or a shamba. In books of education it is always emphasized that supervision should aim at supplying leadership to help the staff to improve the instructional situation.

The challenge to the headteacher in the 1970s

By way of conclusion to this chapter, we would like to say something about the challenge to the head teacher in the 1970s. First of all, there have been winds of change and there is now no place in school administration for an autocratic headmaster or headmistress. He/ she couldn't possibly hold the school together long.

The headmaster has of necessity to share his/ her leadership function with his/ her staff and students. In this decade, although this may not be the case now, the idea of the headteacher commanding authority because of his personal qualities alone will give way to the headteacher whose authority is based on his known professional competence and keen understanding of the role of the school in contemporary society.

The challenge those who become headteachrs face now is simply this, that they have to be aware of and understand the changes going on in education and to be receptive to the ideas themselves. This necessarily requires that the head listens to suggestions from his staff and is prepared to spend as much time as possible in discussion with them. Now that schools are much larger than they used to be, the head has unavoidably to delegate responsibility, accompanied by a considerable degree of freedom, to his colleagues to act on his behalf and he has to be prepared to accept responsibility for the mistakes they make.

Furthermore, in this decade the head will have to keep abreast of information about experiments going on and attend education conferences regularly. Moreover, he must make an effort as he performs his duties to try to visualise the magnitude of the changes which are bound to affect schools sooner or later and the lives of students now at school as members of adult society in the last decades of this century. Hard as it may be the headmaster has to address himself to this challenge.

REFERENCES

Papers

The Phelps-Stokes Report 1923-4, ed. J. Lewis.
Reports of the Education Department and the Ministry of Education 1925-68, Government Printer, Entebbe.
Report on Proceedings of the Legislative Council 1926, Government Printer, Entebbe.
African Education in Uganda... 1953 (the de Bunsen Report), Government Printer, Entebbe, 1953.
The Economic Development of Uganda, International Bank for Reconstruction and Development, Government Printer, Entebbe, 1961.
The Teachers' Salary Report (the Lawrence Report, Government Printer, Entebbe, 1962.
The Board of Governors (Self-Governing Schools) Rules, Government Printer, Entebbe, 1962.
The Education (Teachers' Conditions of Service) Rules, Government Printer, Entebbe 1962.
Proceedings of the Uganda National Assembly, vol. 22, Government Printer, Entebbe, 1963.
Subsidiary Legislation, Statutory Instruments no. 244, 1969.
The Education Management Committees (Amendment) Rules 1969.
Uganda Education Act 1970, Government Printer, Entebbe 1970.

Books

Castle, E.B., *Growing Up in East Africa*, Oxford University Press 1967.
Edel, M.N., *The Kiga of Western Uganda*, Oxford University Press 1957.
Kaggwa, Sir Apolo, *Customs of the Baganda*, trans. E.B. Kalibbala, Columbia University Press, 1934.
Kavulu, D. , *The Uganda Martyrs, Uganda* Publishing House 1970.
Kenyatta, J., *Facing Mount Kenya*, London, Secker and Warburg 1938.
Lawrence, The Iteso, Oxford University Press.
Mbiti, J., *The Akamba Stories*, Clarendon Press 1966.
Oliver, R. *The Missionary Factor in East Africa*, Longmans 1965.
Roscoe, J., *The Baganda*, 2nd ed., London, Frank Cass, 1965 (Simon, H.A., Administrative Behaviour, New York, The Free Press, 1965).

Tucker, A. R., *Eighteen Years in Uganda and East Africa*, London. Edward Arnold 1911.
Welbourne, F.B., *East African Christian*, Oxford University Press 1965.

Articles
Wandira, A., 'Embarrassment: A Spur to Endeavour', The Teacher, 1, 1971, Makerere University Printer.

Appendix A

Directors of Education 1925-62

Mr. Eric R.J. Hussey, M.A. (Oxon), 1925-28.
Mr. E.G. Morris, O.B.E., B.A. (Oxon), 1929-34.
Mr. H.Jowitt, B.A., M. Ed. (S.A.), 1934-45.
Mr. J. R. Cullen, M.A. (Oxon), 1945-52.
Mr. C.R.V. Bell, O.B.E., B.A. (Oxon), June 1958-62.

Chief Education Officers 1962-72

Mr. S.C. Wood, B.A. (Oxon) PGD Ed. 1962-64.
Mr. M.K. Sozi, B.A. (London), M.A. (Hons) Edinburgh),
Dip. Ed. (E.A.), May 1964-68.
Mr. E.K. Sempebwa, B.Sc. (Econ) (London), January 1969-72.

Chief Inspectors of Schools

Mr. R. E. Parry, B.A. (London) 1934.
Mr. R. Snoxall, M.A. (Cantab).
Mr. F.H. Stevens, 1964.
Mr. B. P. Kiwanuka, B.Sc. (Wales), Dip. Ed. 1964-68.
Mr. J. Aryada, M.A. (Oxon), January 1969-72.

Appendix B

Secondary Schools 1972

Schools with S1-S6 Classes
Aga khan Secondary School, Kampala
Kibuli Secondary School, Kampala
Kololo Secondary School, Kampala
Makerere College School, Kampala
Old Kampala Secondary School, Kampala
Namagunga, Mount St. Mary's Secondary School
Namilyango College
Budo King's College
Gayaza High School
Kisubi St. Mary's College
Nabbingo Trinity College
Mbale Secondary School

Nabumali High School
Tororo St. Peter's College
Tororo Girls' School
Jinja Secondary School
Busoga College, Mwiri
Teso College, Aloet
Kitgum High School
Sir Samuel Baker School
Boroboro Secondary School
Lango College
Mvara Secondary School
Ntare School, Mbarara
Kabalega Secondary School
Kigezi High School
Nyakasura School

Schools with S1-S4 Classes

Kitante Hill Secondary School, Kampala
Kyambogo College School, Kampala
Lubiri Secondary School, Kampala
Mengo Secondary School, Kampala
Nabisunsa Girls Secondary School, Kampala
Mukono Bishop's Senior Secondary School
Ndejje Secondary School
Aga khan Masaka Secondary School
Kako Secondary School
Christ The King Girls' Secondary School, Kalisizo
Masaba Secondary School
Nkoma Secondary School
Kachonga, Bukedi College
Manjasi High School
Kiira College, Butiki
Iganga Secondary School
Jinja College
Parvatiben Muljibhai Madhvani Girls' School
Madhvani College, Wairaka
Wanyange Busoga College
Tegres Sebei Secondary School
Ngora High School
Gulu High School

St. Joseph's College, Layibi
Sacred Heart Girls' School
Moroto High School
Comboni College, Ngetta
St. Katherine's School
Moyo Secondary School
St. Charles Lwanga College, Koboko
St. Aloysius College, Nyapea
St. Joseph's College, Ombaci
Bweranyangi Girls' Secondary School
Ibanda Secondary School
Kitunga High School
Mary-Hill High School
Mbarara High School
St. Edward's Secondary School, Bukumi
Duhaga Secondary School, Hoima
Kigezi College, Butobere
Makobore High School, Kinyasano
Mutolere Secondary School
Kyebambe Girls' Secondary School
St. Leo's College, Kyegobe

Index

African School Teachers Association (A.S.T.A.) 51
Agricultural 4, 6, 10, 35, 38, 60
  Colleges 35, 60
  Officer 6
Agriculture 5, 6, 7, 11, 13, 14, 15, 56, 60, 67
  Department 10
  Director of .6
Archer, Geoffrey Sir 4

Bachelor of Education 33
Balintuma, Ernest Kalibbala 43
Board of Governors 10, 11, 16, 70, 71, 79, 86, 87, 88, 94
British Examining Bodies 12
Bursar 88

Cambridge Overseas Examinations Syndicate 38
Cambridge School Certificate 11, 14
Castle Report 17, 19, 38
Catechism 25, 39
Catholic 2, 8, 9, 17, 18, 2 4, 25, 28, 42, 49, 51
  Mission schools 9
  Teachers guild 51
Central schools 2, 5, 7
Chief Education Officer 16, 18, 66, 71, 72, 75, 76, 77, 78
Chief Inspector of Schools 4, 67, 69, 73, 80
Church Missionary Society (CMS) 9, 42
Church of Uganda 28
Civil Service 65, 87
Cohen, Andrew 45
Colonial policy 6
Curriculum Development Centre 37

de Bunsen Committee 15, 16, 29
de la War Commission 14
Department of Education 3, 4, 5, 6, 8, 9, 26, 28, 38, 47
Director of Education 4, 5, 6, 8, 10, 11, 26
District Education 72
  Committee 28, 72
  Offices 18, 71
  Officer 72

East African School Leaving Examination 12
Education 1, 2, 3, 4, 5, 6, 7, 8, 9, 10, 11-18, 21, 22, 26-28, 32, 33, 35-38, 47, 53, 56, 60, 65, 66, 67, 68, 69, 71, 72- 80, 85-90, 94, 96
  Administration of 64, 65, 68, 71, 72
  Bill 5
  Legal framework of 73
  Committee 28, 72
  Native 5, 23, 28, 44
  Policy 10, 17
  White Paper 4, 56
Education 1945 - 62 15
Education Act 1970 66, 69, 71, 73, 74, 79, 80, 94
Education Ordinance 1927 5
  1942 10
  1959 16
Education since 1962 16
Education system 3, 5, 6, 9, 31, 38, 56, 59, 61, 62, 63
  Structure of 16
Elementary Vernacular schools 5, 6, 7
Examination 12, 14, 15, 60, 58, 67, 70, 76, 77, 89, 90

External 89
Internal 89

Farm School 9
Father Spartas 43

Government 4
Grade 3 teacher 30
Graduate teacher 33

Head teacher 90, 91, 92
  Challenge to 92
Higher Education 11, 12, 13, 15, 66
  Division 66
Higher School Certificate 19, 32, 35, 60
Hussey, Eric 7

Inspection 11
  Forms of 69
  Full 70
  Why Inspect 68
  Pastoral or advisory 70
  Partial 71
Inspector of Schools 4, 67, 66, 69, 70, 71, 73, 80
  Powers of 69
Inter-University Council 14
Invigilator 90

Junior Secondary School 8, 27

Kabaka's Government 18
Kiswahili 7, 8, 9, 27

Legislative Council 5, 6, 94
Local Government Councils 45

Makerere 2, 3, 5, 8, 10-15, 19, 27, 28, 30, 32, 33, 34, 35, 36, 38, 41, 43, 44, 49, 52, 60, 61, 62, 71, 95, 96
  Academic Board 14
  College 5, 8, 11, 12, 13, 14, 15, 27, 28, 30, 32, 44, 96
  University College 15
  University Kampala 27
  Technical Schools 5, 8, 17, 20
Makerere College Act 14
Makerere College Ordinance of 1938 13
Makerere Technical College 41
Maternity schools 2
Mill Hill Fathers 2
Ministry of Education 33, 37, 47, 53, 65, 67, 68, 72, 74, 75, 80, 85, 86, 87, 89, 90, 94
mission schools 3, 4, 7, 9, 24, 25, 43, 44, 71
Missionaries 2, 3, 4, 5, 7, 9, 22, 23, 24, 25, 26, 27, 40, 41, 42, 43, 45, 49, 51
  Contribution to education 3
  Groups 2
Mukasa, Ssebbanja 43
Musoke, Anselm 43
Muslim schools 43

National Teachers College, Kyambogo 33
  Native 5, 23, 28, 44
  Anglican Church 28
  Native Education 5
  Teachers 23
Normal schools 2, 5, 8, 26
Nyanjeeradde 27

Peace Corps 36
  Scheme 36
  Teachers 36

Phelps-Stokes 2, 3, 4, 94
   Commission 2, 3, 4
   Fund 3
Post Primary 17, 58. *See also* secondary
   schools
Prefects 85
Primary Leaving Examination 58, 67
Primary School 8, 17, 25, 26, 30, 35,
   40, 48, 49, 56, 57, 58, 69, 73
   Leavers 17, 56, 57
Private schools 19, 35, 43, 66, 73, 74
Professional relations 22, 34
Protectorate Government 2, 3, 4, 6
Protestant Missions 17

Religious knowledge 2
Roman Catholic 24, 25, 28, 42, 49

Scheme of work 31, 70, 90, 91
Schools and Colleges 37, 66, 67
   Division 66
   Inspectorate Division 67
Secondary School 8, 13, 28, 27, 33,
   34, 52, 57, 58, 59, 60, 82, 83,
   85, 86, 88, 89, 96, 97, 98
Senior Secondary School 8, 13, 52, 97
   Administration 82
Staff meetings 85, 91, 92
Supervision 2, 3, 6, 17, 32, 73, 85,
   89, 90, 91, 92

Teacher and the law 74, 75
Teacher education 11, 13, 21, 22, 26,
   33, 36, 37, 38, 56, 60, 66, 74
   Government participation in 4
   Development of 21
Teachers 2, 5, 6, 7, 9, 10, 12, 14,
   15, 16, 18, 22-38, 40-54, 56,
   61, 66-75, 81, 82, 83, 84, 8-92
   Colleges 27, 36, 42, 52
   Graduate expatriate 36
   Training schools 26, 28, 42, 52

Teachers for East Africa (T.E.A) 36
Teaching Service Commission
   53, 77, 78
Technical Schools 5, 8, 17, 20
Tucker, Alfred Bishop 24
Institute of Education, the 37, 38

Uganda African Teachers Association
   (U.A.T.A.) 50
Uganda College of Commerce 20
Uganda Muslim Education
   Association 17, 18
Uganda Railways 6
Uganda Teachers Association
   51, 52, 53
Uganda Teachers Union 52, 53
University 12, 13, 14, 15, 16,
   19, 27, 34, 36, 38, 56,
   60, 61, 62, 65, 66,
   71, 89, 94, 95
   College 13, 14, 15, 38
   For East Africa 38
   Teachers 15, 22, 33,
      34, 35, 36, 39,
      43, 50, 51, 52,
      53, 54, 60, 75, 89, 90

Vernacular 5,
   6, 7, 9, 26, 27, 28, 30, 52
   Teacher Training Centres 27
   Teachers 27, 30
   Schools 5, 6, 7
Vernacular Primary and Junior
   Teachers Association 52
Vocational 6, 8,
   7, 12, 17, 56, 58, 60, 62
   Courses 7
   Programmes 60
   Vocational training 7, 12, 56

White paper. *See also* Education

www.ingramcontent.com/pod-product-compliance
Lightning Source LLC
Chambersburg PA
CBHW071409290426
44108CB00014B/1745